Safari West

Mary Hocking

Churchtown Technology
St. Buryan — Cornwall

Safari West

July 1996

ISBN 0-9527556-0-2

Design and illustration by
Churchtown Technology, St. Buryan
Printing by Headland Printers, Penzance

Published on
behalf of the author by
Churchtown Technology
Sunny Corner, Galligan Lane
St. Buryan, PENZANCE
Cornwall, TR19 6BY
ENGLAND

Preface

I first visited West Penwith over thirty years ago. Although I was brought up on the River Fal, I had never ventured west of Penzance before being summoned to tea by my prospective parents-in-law. As my ancient and unreliable car plunged down the hill past Trereife, I can still remember the sense of entering a magical kingdom, quite removing my apprehensions about what lay ahead. This sense of wonder is still with me. Mary Hocking's book about West Penwith and its people helps to explain why this is such a special place.

In a world where so much seems to be changing, and for the worst, it is surely a comfort to know that the spirit of community, that has always characterised the south west tip of Cornwall, endures. It is a spirit forged by hardship: at sea, down the mines and on the land. Today – the tin mines are museums; the fishing fleet faces an uncertain future; the rural economy is under threat and the preservation of the local environment from the pressure of development is a constant challenge. Fortunately the community spirit of earlier times lives on and Mary Hocking's stories will help to ensure that it is passed on to future generations.

Safari West will, I am sure, delight local people & visitors alike.

Sir John Banham
West Penwith

Safari West

St. Just

Aerodrome

Carn Euny

Chapel Carn Brea

Crow-an-Wra

A30

Boscarn

(Gwenver)

Escalls

Sunny Corner

Rissick

Sennen Cove

Mayon

St. Sennen

PENROSE

St. Buryan

Alsia

Goonmenheere

(well)

B3283

Land's End   A30

Trevilley   B3315   Trengothal

Crean

Bottoms

Tresidder

Nanjizel   Polgigga

Trethewey   B3315

Trendrennen

Silena

Burnewhall

Boscean

Treen   Penberth

Porthcurno

Logan Rock

St. Levan

The Minack

Porthgwarra

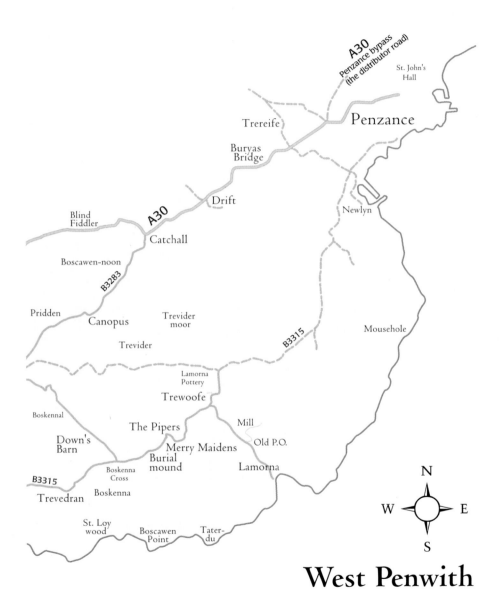

West Penwith

Contents:

Introduction

"**Safari West**" began through my childrens' questions on the truth behind the tales that I was recalling to them - just as my grandmother had passed to me some years before.

In the quest to obtain what truth could be found much of our cultural heritage came forward. These last three parishes of Cornwall - St. Buryan, St. Levan and St. Sennen - with much to be remembered and some still left intact, it all just had to be collated.

now known as Sennen

The tales also intermingle in a jigsaw effect, which led me to write as if I were taking you on walks. Beginning with the Rev. Spry, our first character of great humour, who leads us from St. John's Hall steps in Penzance onto our Safari West. There's a map on pages 4 & 5. You may like to follow our trail pinpointing the various exploits of the tales.

Much of the land and moorlands are unchanged, which is fortunate, and have escaped from undue modern development.

There are cliff walks from Lamorna, to Land's End and on around to Sennen. Tales of smugglers, romance and intrigue. So too there are ghost tales and even apparitions, of which people have told me where and what they had seen.

Boscawen Point near Lamorna

This far western part of Penwith is truly an area of immeasurable interest.

Safari West

ST. JOHN'S HALL
— *found on the high
side of Penzance
along Alverton Street*

Let's start our safari, shooting with a camera or sketch pad, from the ST. JOHN'S HALL. The granite steps — this hard silver grey stone for which Cornwall is renown and of which most of this building has been built. One such step is over 17ft long and all were quarried at Lamorna. The old photograph shows how it used to look. It is a valley which we shall visit later. Can you imagine the hauling of such a stone, from the cliff in a little cove, to the boat and reversing the system at the sea-front, then to be hauled by horses and men to its final position?

There it stands as good as new - even today. The sheer weight of one such stone must be quite immense.

*down the Hall's steps
turn right (west)
and across the
roundabout
& then look right…*

Now in the footsteps of the Rev. Spry - there are several cottages past the entrance of the 'Hollies' [a private house]. Our Rev. Spry is thought to have lived in one of these cottages and was curate of St. Levan & Sennen 1816-1826. He was a character of outrageous dress, with a sense of fun and loved to chatter loudly, even to repeat jokes that had counted against himself.

Market day

This incident occurred near the *Pirate Inn*, over a little stream which formed a simple ford across the road in those days. One Thursday morning market day, many farmers' wives had gathered on their way to the market astride their horses and ponies whatever. Their loaded baskets were upon their knees so as to relax their arms and, with the reins left loose, the horses had a well-earned drink before entering into the bustle of the town. On this particular day, a peaceful sunny scene, there was to be heard only the sounds of birds singing and of the ladies' cheerful chatter.

continue straight on; over another small roundabout; the Pirate Inn can be seen on the left as the road starts to climb

Suddenly along comes our Rev. Spry in his outrageous attire freewheeling down around the corner at great speed upon his VELOCIPEDE — the only one in the area at this time. Too late he realises he would not stop in time. It's into the ladies, water and horses went he. Flying went the eggs and floating went the butter. Splash went our parson — for no brakes had his 'steed' — so no hope of escape from this disaster.

VELOCIPEDE — *an early wooden tricycle in this case*

While those ladies who were thrown from their horses were in this whirlpool of water and mud they quite forgot their manners and did pelt the parson with all they could — not forgetting the eggs. It is said they half-killed the man and he was lucky some gentlemen came to his aid to rescue both man and wooden steed. By now many of the horses were out of sight — some gone home, others into town to where they were regularly stabled on a market day.

The following Sunday he was unable to attend to his duties! People, hoping to see how the parson had fared, had congregated along the road and up Rospletha Hill at Porthcurno near St. Levan Church. In fact these folks, waiting on most roads west, were left disappointed.

This story – being of a pure accident – is surely the type of position in which only the Rev. Spry could find himself. While the next story tells us how the mischievous pranks he would get up to.

Our racing Rev. Spry on Tul-tuf hill

TUL-TUF HILL – *just a little way along the road from the last tale*

He was very proud of his wooden steed, even more so when he found it would run downhill with so much speed.

On yet another market day, early in the morning, the parson stationed himself, ready mounted, to challenge anybody coming from, or going to, the market. Eager for a race but always *down* the hill be-it-understood! Plenty of farmers desired no better fun than to wager a race with the man on this new fandangle.

The unfortunate nags were not knowing what to make of this parson's queer beast going on three wheels and like the wind. In their fears and doubts about the nature of the thing, they either sprang over the nearest hedge or threw their masters into ditches - just so that they might be overtaken by this most unnatural object. So for a long time did the parson boast often and loudly how his 'horse' was the fastest in the West.

(at the top of the hill turn left at the A30 roundabout & signed Land's End)

This man will appear again along our trail.

The Tree Lined Avenue

On going through the avenue of trees at the Trereife crossroad, when it was but a width of a cart track, may I remind you of what my great-aunt Ethel said to her future husband and is so very true even today.

the area of Trereife is up to the right

"Now Asa, take a real good look at these here trees, for they will be the most you'll see together 'til you get back here again."

They were travelling to Trengothal Farm and he was from the Truro area - more noted for forestry.

It is here at this spot that the campus for the University of Cornwall is expected to be centred. Penwith won the bid to build and host it, when the University of Exeter put out their prospectus.

Buryas Bridge

*when the road opens
out into a valley, the
garage is to the right*

As you drive slowly past, you may be able to recognise what used to be the old *First and Last Garage*, although it is in fact at Buryas Bridge – some seven miles from Land's End.

Maybe the people of the 1920's did not expect the car to become so popular. The road had to be widened to such a degree that we have lost a lovely picturesque humpback bridge and the view of the river. Since the building of the dam and reservoir at nearby Drift, the river has become the overflow and continues through the valley to meet the sea at Newlyn. The dam is on plain view just a little way through this next hamlet of Drift. I believe fishing permits may be available.

*to detour to see the
dam turn right at
Drift - it is not far*

The Days of the Horse

*at Catchall turn left
on the B3283*

We get off the main A30 road by turning left and are now travelling along a side road – heading towards St. Buryan.

To the right is Trenuggo. Here on this farm is the BLIND FIDDLER – standing at an angle in a field. Like the 'Merry Maidens' (which we will come to later) it is said to be a petrified reveller of the Sabbath. The noted archeologist W.C. Borlase said of this place:

BLIND FIDDLER –
*a long upright stone
made of granite (not
visible from this road)*

"A man seeking treasure here found only bones and ashes".

Trenuggo still has many splendid shire horses which used to do much of the farm work. It's been my luck while passing to watch these gentle giants plant their feet with such firmness, while their shoulders' strength pulled the implement forward with unbelievable ease. Their FEATHERS and light fluffy manes flowed in the wind. The sheen of their coats gleamed in the sunshine as the shires moved ever forward.

FEATHERS — *long hairs on the shire horses' legs*

Further along we come to Trelew, a hill that travellers dreaded in my grandmother's day. As horses lost their speed up the hill, rogues and thieves took advantage. Many were robbed.

At the top of this hill is the farm of Toldavus. At this farm the tenant Mr. L. Pengelly met his death just a few years ago by an accident with an electric mill. He was a man of whom I only heard good spoken. A quiet unassuming man who did much good in so many ways.

In that farm lane there is a large boulder. It was discovered in the exploring of *Lockyer's November Sunrise Line* from Boscawn-un Circle past Stone 6 at Trelew – as John Michell reports in his book *The Old Stones of Land's End* [1]. It is one I would recommend to any student of the megalithic science.

Opposite the farm entrance of Toldavus is the Trelew Farm entrance and on this farm a tall stone stands. When W.C. Borlase excavated this site, he found wood, flint clay, and human bones so strongly cemented together that the workmen declared they were set in lime.

at Canopus

Down to the next coppice. We cross a river, which is the one said to have seen a battle of such slaughter that the mill was worked by the blood that flowed. This roughly sketched map shows some interesting points about the immediate area.

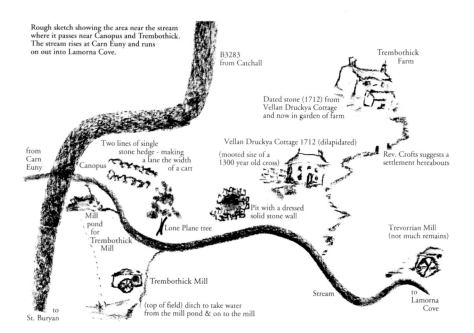

Rough sketch showing the area near the stream where it passes near Canopus and Trembothick. The stream rises at Carn Euny and runs on out into Lamorna Cove.

B3283 from Catchall

Trembothick Farm

Dated stone (1712) from Vellan Druckya Cottage and now in garden of farm

Vellan Druckya Cottage 1712 (dilapidated)

Two lines of single stone hedge - making a lane the width of a cart

from Carn Euny

Canopus

(mooted site of a 1300 year old cross)

Rev. Crofts suggests a settlement hereabouts

Pit with a dressed solid stone wall

Mill pond for Trembothick Mill

Lone Plane tree

Trevorrian Mill (not much remains)

Trembothick Mill

(top of field) ditch to take water from the mill pond & on to the mill

Stream

to St. Buryan

to Lamorna Cove

Vellan-Drucke (Trembothick)

This sketch is taken from a € map, with the river rising at
Carn Euny and meeting the sea at Lamorna.

VELLANDRUCHER
means *wheel mill*, also
suggesting an apparatus
driven by water surges
– so I've been given to
understand.

The Cornish gave the
name MELYN-DRUCKY
or VELYN-DRUCKYA to
the mills used to dip,
clean and dress their
home spun cloth. A
cloth mill can also be
called FULLER, TUCKER,
TROCHIER. I would like

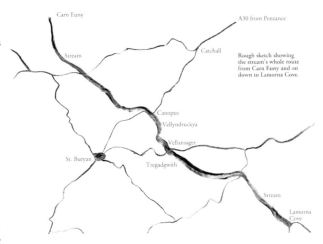

Rough sketch showing
the stream's whole route
from Carn Euny and on
down to Lamorna Cove.

to have found some evidence of flax grown for linen but have
not done so yet, so must assume these mills were used in the
processing of wool fabric.

Here is that river that is
said to have flowed with
enough blood of the
Danes to run a mill after
a battle with legendary
King Arthur. Remains of
weapons, similar to those
which would have been
used in early times, have
been found in the
moorland peat:

    eg arrow, spear &
      also axe heads.

The Pot and the Adders

The moors about do unfortunately accommodate adders.
It was said that the Trembothick moor was so infested with
adders that no cattle could be turned onto it in the summer.

One day a man, who was cutting the peat turf on the moor,
went to his pot of milk he had placed in the shade for his
refreshment. To his surprise an adder had won him to it.

He placed a large turf upon the receptacle which stopped the
adder getting away. The adder then gave out a most peculiar
noise, which attracted more adders around the pot. These in
their turn seemed to call others until, from all parts of the
moor, they had slithered in a straight course and enclasped,
one and all, into a solid heap around the captive and pot.

FURZE — *cut down
'gorse bush' (see also
page 143)*

HAYCOCK — *pile of
loose hay roughly a
yard high and again
across*

It did not take long, either for the man to call the other men
on the moor to depart until eventide, or to decide a plan of
action. They decided to place FURZE around the adder pile
which was said by then to have been the size of a large
HAYCOCK. They had been cutting peat for the winter's fuel,
so they also put this on top of the furze and set it all alight.
The noise made by these creatures was said to be horrendous
and frightening. Similar stories to this have been told of
other moors in the area.

The last farmstead on your right, before you enter the
village of St. Buryan, is called Pridden. Near to the front
of the farmhouse a large stone stands at a precarious angle
right at the end of a field's hedge. This stone's base was
excavated by the well known W.C. Borlase. Apparently a
sketch of his showed how the hedge had, at one time, been
built around this particular stone. His find was of some
human bones at the south side.

St. Buryan

Enter St. Buryan, the historic village, whose centre we will cross again and again. So many authors have mentioned it in numerous books — as you will see when you compare that information against the little which I've found written of St. Levan and St. Sennen.

commonly Sennen

The Chapel

The Methodist Chapel was rebuilt in 1981. I feel you will agree that it is of a fine modern design, both inside & out, giving the illusion of space. The picture shows it at the turn of the century when it had a further storey.

to your left a little way into the village

From our own Mr. J.M. Hosking's book *Methodism in St. Buryan* [2] you can obtain all the possible facts I would think one could wish to know of Methodism in this area. It is from this book we find something of the ancestry of John Wesley, whose mother was a strong influence in his life. Wesley was one of the fifth generation, as recorded in this book, to struggle in the cause of his religion, which he endeavoured to do with amazing success.

> "Tradition has it that he used the Mounting Block for this purpose…" [ie as a pulpit]

In 1766, on Sunday 7th September, Wesley mentioned in his diary that he was:

"...preaching at Mousehole, thence to St. Buryan"

It is possible that this was to occur in the church, as the Rev. Robert Coker (a man who had ridiculed him on an earlier occasion) was dead.

We read of Meeting houses becoming so full that the further building of chapels became necessary. Then, as those not being big enough, even bigger chapels were built. It was altered in 1908 and closed because of storm damage in 1976. This was the one that I attended for Sunday School.

At the Sunday School

BANK OF HOPE –
a happy procession
of the children

I suppose about 40 children were in the line to march through the village at the BAND OF HOPE. When sports were the order of the day, Sid Lugg sold his home-made ice cream. Darn-me, I've tried making this, but could not get it to taste like his. Sometimes Leslie Payne would set up a little tent to sell sweets. I don't ever remember rain on this day, but knowing the organisers of the time, they'd probably arranged

indoor games. We would not have noticed. Then we'd have a Tea, where all sat on long forms and Grace said. The older children down to the very young tackled the saffron buns which would be about six inches across. There would be other cakes of a plain nature on the table - Cornish SPLITS with plenty of butter and some with cream and a dob of jam. Few would be touched as the saffron bun filled most of us.

SPLITS — fancy bread rolls

My days at the Sunday School Treat were soon after the war, which I suppose was why only plain cakes were the order of the day.

WWII

I remember the Sunday School afternoons always had cheerful Hymns and the stories of the Bible were kept simple so that we should understand the full meaning of the parable.

On special occasions like anniversaries we were allowed into the front to recite our recitations. We always walked through, from the Sunday School rooms into the Chapel, with such a reverence as children today appear not to know. There was no chatter, giggling or wriggling. The vastness of the place, with the gallery around in a semi-circle, made a daunting sight. We sat proudly and in sheer awe of the honour of sitting next to the preacher in the pulpit – which had steps either side.

Lisbon Terrace

As you enter the village of St. Buryan the road branching to the right takes you past Lisbon Terrace. The end house has a stone dated 1823. Beside is the site of the remains of the Bible Christian Chapel which was opened 1860 and closed in 1932, as a result of the union with the Methodist Church.

(far end)

St. Buryan Church

While in this frame of mind let's consider the
St. Buryan Parish Church. On this mound
King Athelstan is said to have first seen the
Isles of Scilly and vowed, if he were to be
successful in conquering those Islands,
he would endow a church at St. Buryan.
The next day he set sail from Sennen. We
have proof of his success by the way of a
Charter dated October 932, which has
been translated and a copy stands within
the church for anyone to read – along with a
full list of deans and rectors over the years.

More on St. Buryan and its church later.

Out into my country

Straight through the village, on the
Porthcurno road for about half a mile, you
will come to the *Goonmenheere* stile on the
right hand side. This has a meaning in
Cornish of a large stone, as I understand.
Over the stile across the field to the valley
of Alsia. We are now off into the country
where it's so easy to imagine oneself in a
world on your own - with only nature's noises
and the occasional car to disturb your dreams.
The flowers of the wayside 'wave and smile' in
colours clear, oh so clear, as but few can paint.
The delicate reds and pinks of the red campion, the
strong yellow peeping around the prickle of the gorse,
or the tufted vetch winding itself this way and that.

This is my home area that I know and love so well. As many as 50 species of plants I've found in the month of February in the lane of Higher Alsia. The number must be quite phenomenal in late spring & early summer. Only recently I've been told by experts there are some 120 different grasses in Cornwall.

The inland birds - just you sit and listen, not as much singing as chattering amongst themselves. There must be an incredible number of common birds also. In this part of my Cornwall the jay has come to visit us in only the last few years. His habits, as I've read of 'a liking for the eggs of other birds', have quite put me off looking forward to seeing them. One has to admit though, such colourful plumage is a splendid work of art. A hoopoe has also been seen here in the last few years but only very rarely. His crest of feathers look so much like that of a cock-a-too.

The evening and night time is for those numerous bats that appear to be aiming at you but never hit you. Dusk descends. One can often hear the barn owl hooting through the dark hours. Its snowy white feathers, partially covered with a delicate laced golden pattern, have to be seen at close quarters to be appreciated.

The woodpecker lives here which one might not expect, when you see we have more

DUTCH ELM –
*an epidemic that just
about wiped out all
existing elms*

bushes than trees. It was so before the dreaded DUTCH ELM. Only now can you see the full extent of the damage that this wrought through, not only our lovely valley, but also Lamorna and the Bottoms valley areas. Now they are devoid of all but a few of their erstwhile towering giants. Speaking to many farmers and their helpers, I am told of the creeks and vales – hidden from general view – that are in the same devastation.

Baker's Downs

From an old Ordnance Survey map [3] the Field N° 1594 and possibly N° 1602 (today called Baker's Downs field) were both of rough downland, whence they got their name.

From the story Miss Ethel Thomas had often told me...
  "It was a fine day, when the Baker in his cart rode by, as I've been told years ago," says she "that up the road did trot - and for no reason known to man - the 'osse took it into his head to gallop, way down through the moor, straight into the mine shaft which is said to be as deep as the church tower is high."   [92ft]

The site number of this shaft is N° 1593. We have never found any tool of any sort, though many loads of earth as fine as powder have been carried to other parts of the farm. I've heard it said this mine was worked in 1510, but have yet to find papers to confirm it. Mining in this parish has been noted also at Pendrea, Selena, Tresidder, Trelew, Boleigh, Cardinney, Boscarn and Lefra but that little, if any, is thought to go underground.

Around this shaft at Alsia are little meadows. In about 1947 my father imported bulbs of the Narcissus family from Holland and had the small meadows brought into production by men using shovels. Many of the meadows still have the flowers in them, even with no attention being given to them in these past decades.

Alsia Mill

The river in this valley holds a book full of stories, as much of my early days were spent there with my sisters. No matter what the weather, or the time of year, we would run down from the farm on the hill, or sometimes *roly-poly* down.

Then calling into the cottage to chat with Mrs. Greet, who had the patience of a saint, what with our eternal questions on whatever she might be making. There was always something - whether knitting, sewing or baking. Sometimes we'd be just in time for TATTIE CAKE just out of the oven of the tiny Cornish range, with the black of the stove shining as much as its brasses. Then it was over the little stream to help [!] Miss Ethel Thomas or her brother Thornley. These people had such patience with us - it's quite unbelievable, as I can assure you we were a very questioning gang of three and needed to know the *why's and what for's* of everything. Perhaps, as most of my young days were of wartime and just after, we gave hope to their future.

TATTIE CAKE — *potato cake*

The river in summer was but a trickle, but in winter it would thunder over the millwheel with an almighty crashing noise over which you could not hear yourself speak — speeding down the race by our feet. There was no rail or concrete blocks for our safety and you can bet we took no risks such as people do today. Whenever they see a safety rail they have a habit of leaning on it. While the thundering waterfall was going on outside, Mr. Thomas would be in the mill grinding the corn (only for his own use as I understand). Inside it was quite silent but for the mild creaking of the cogs and the slither of the bags as they were drawn into place. The difference in sound inside and out was quite unbelievable. The mill wheel stopped in the '60s when he got an electric machine to do the work.

*at Alsia Mill's race —
myself, sister Joyce &
my twin Margaret
(a few months later
Margaret died of
complications after
a hospital visit)*

We watched the slim black trout and tried to catch them
with crudely made hooks. Remember, girls were not supposed
to be interested in such boyish ways then, so we got no
encouragement to improve our methods. Along the river bank
we spent hours, with some success, trapped some voles in jam
jars — temporarily you understand.

This valley has been described as one of the most beautiful
places to be seen in the parish of St. Buryan. In the 1850's,
when surrounded with orchards in full blossom, W. Bottrell
describes in his book [4] :

> "A cottage above the mill so full of every perfumed flowers and
> herbs, for the use of medicine and for the bees to make the honey."

The Well story

The well is some 300 yards from Alsia Mill and farmyard.
It has never been known to run dry in its centuries old life.
Children were bathed in its water to *help* cure rickets.
Miss Thomas told me maidens would throw in pins and make
wishes to marry the man of their choice. Valley women fought
to keep people away from their drinking water. She also said
that it was reputed to be the coldest well in the parish and
reminisced of carrying the cream to be cooled, so that it could
be turned into butter, during the very hot summers.

It has seen many changes and still has a spiritual attraction.
This year an idol has been placed along with ribbons in the
tree which hangs over the well – even money (a new idea).
I feel all this activity rather sad. The ribbons, for instance,
will become unwelcome debris to the area and the coins
could pollute the purity of the water.

*go past Alsia Farm's
entrance; down into
the valley, just after
climbing out there is
a farm gate on the
left; make your way
across and onwards
through to the next
field; head half-right
down the rolling hill;
the well is to be
found on the right
near the bottom*

returning to the road

The Story of Penrose Manor

continue for ⅔ᵈ mile; road drops sharply and Penrose gateway is on the left near the bottom of that valley

GWENVER — more commonly; OS map refers to Gywnver

This lovely house of Penrose Manor [a listed building] has many stories to tell. Although but a shadow of its former self it has the elegant appearance of a long forgotten past. The valley leads to Penberth about three miles away. One can walk that way even now and, at one time, this must have aided the smuggler greatly. So to, in the opposite direction from the house, a path leads over the fields and moor to GWENVER sands adjoining Whitesand Bay beach or Sennen Beach as it is more often called today.

There are mysterious enough looking buildings adjoining the house, but it is the old house which most persons even today regard with a degree of interest that no modern structure can command. With well faced stone and mullioned windows, its massive chimneys and the front garden are set among high walls on three sides.

During the early part of ℭ, when it was still the home of the Penrose family, we gather from tales told at the fireside during long winter evenings that a squire of Penrose had brought up one of his sons as a seafarer. This life he continued to follow until his older brothers died – leaving him heir to the family estate.

Loving the sea as he did, he spent little time on the estate but with his well armed, fast, sailing craft which was ideal for smuggling, or *fair trading* as they would prefer to have us believe. Privateer and pirate meant very much the same in those days. She was manned with a brave crew, most of whom were said to be the squire's poor relations. A favourite cousin being William Penrose – a shipmate of many years.

The new seafarer squire often took trips to France and other places. This crew are known to have spent little time ashore except in the dead of winter. Yet life in the squire's house was always furnished with good substantial fare. Food was plentiful and with the best liquors – free for all comers. Unfortunately this happy state only lasted a few years, as the squire was left a widower with a son about 7 years of age. This man seemed to hate even the sight of land now, so with his young son, his cousin William and two or three old sailors he would stay out at sea for weeks at a time – even in the dead of winter. As usual he left the care of the estate and household to a younger brother and an old steward.

On returning from one of these trips, on a dark winter's night, their boat struck on the Cowloe rock and became a wreck. He swam into Sennen Cove with his young lad and returned, with endeavour, to save others of his crew but got himself drowned in the attempt.

Now the only original brother remaining was Jan [John]. He constituted himself sole guardian of the heir and therefore master of the place and property. Jan had taken to dislike all that his brother had favoured and in consequence the cousin William left the West, it was thought for a life at sea.

Jan got a smuggling craft and manned her with a crew who cared little what they did for their gold or excitement. Well armed they feared little of what sailed on the ocean. He never went to sea himself but left a wretch of a man in command – well known as a pirate. This motley crew boarded

many a rich merchant ship going up the Channel, from which
they took just whatever they pleased before sending all who
opposed them to a watery grave. There was no policing of the
seas in those days, or not of strength to meet such gangs.
If Revenue cutters came near our western land their crews
dreaded to fall in with the Cornish *fair traders* – more than
our smugglers feared the King's men. As for Revenue riding
officers, well they would ride anywhere else rather than on
the cliff when the beacon fires blazed from the cairns – of a
dark night – to guide *fair traders'* boats back into the coves.

When silks, good wines and rich foods were landed and stored
away – much in the vaults of Penrose – it is said that people
came from all over the country to purchase. Apparently the
local youngsters and this crew spent much of their time in a
drunken state during the winter.

The young son of the late good squire seemed instinctively
to avoid this uncle and his hired captain, who consorted
much together when the smugglers were ashore.

Whenever the boy could elude the old steward's vigilance he
would go away to the rocks of Sennen where his father had
drowned, shut himself up for hours in his father's bedroom,
or wander about in the gloomy north wing of the house – a
wing seldom entered by anyone else.

The Hunt

One day in winter, the ground being covered with snow,
Penrose's people and its neighbours joined for a wolf hunt.
Wolves, it is said, were roaming in great numbers during the
1600's and caused havoc with poultry, cattle and had even
been known to carry off children when hard pressed.

On this occasion neither Jan Penrose nor the captain left the homestead. At night the game laden hunters returned up the lane and into the sight of the front of the house with bugle horns blowing. When entering the small courtyard to the right of the house it was, with surprise, that they remarked: "Where's our lad?"

Now the young heir was a general favourite and, normally, he would meet them at the entrance after a hunt. The boy was sought in every place they could imagine. Where else could he be? His uncle seemed quite distressed. Later it was surmised that the child might have wandered under the cliffs at Escalls, thereby got drowned, and was carried out to sea by the ebb tide.

The heir was not found, so now Jan Penrose had all the estate. He became riotously debauched and, apparently, his gang took a strange aversion to the pirate captain. This man then left and was seen no more – hereabouts in the far west.

Strange happenings

The north wing and its tapestry chamber were now shut up, having acquired a reputation for being haunted. Not even the smugglers would venture into it after nightfall. Unearthly shrieks could be heard and strange lights seen flashing through the window until near morning. Lights were also to be seen in the orchard and no one was to be found there.

By way of fun, the Penrose band of villains frequently disguised themselves and made nocturnal excursions to neighbouring villages. There they would alarm the quiet folks in the dead of night by using a volley of firearms, or making a bonfire of furze or even a thatched dwelling!

These frightened people blamed the Spaniards, as they had had a fondness of roving round the coasts and often did much damage in those defenceless places. A few of these dons, sailing at the dead of night into Whitesand Bay and landing on Gwenver sands, are said to have destroyed Vellandreath mill. At the height of such fright and confusion they would carry off such young women as had been agreed on. These ruffians would take the fair ones before them on horseback to places like the Escalls cliff or the hills. They would be left alone at daybreak to find their own way back home on foot.

The people of Buryan's Churchtown had had enough of the Penrose gang. When the men of Buryan heard of another visit, they boldly planned a counter-attack and thus prepared a *warm* reception. As soon as the smuggler gang arrived at the cross, our Buryan men surrounded them. The gang fought desperately, until every man was either killed or disabled. They continued shouting to each other:
  "…cheer up comrades, die one, die all & die we merrily!"

And that was the end of the Penrose gang.

Christmastide at Penrose Manor

The following Christmas, after a day's hunting, a large number of people were enjoying the festivities, when a loud knock came at the green court door. In came an elderly man of untidy appearance asking shelter for the night from the snow storm. He was received with courtesy and, after enjoying the evening entertainment, the steward showed him to a room in the north wing of the house [as the remainder of the house was occupied]. This man seemed not too weary of examining the old portraits, the tapestries, the massive oak furniture with bold grotesque carvings, the ancient armour, coats of arms and other interesting objects. It was about midnight before the traveller settled himself in the window seat.

The scene upon which he cast his eyes was of a snow covered countryside glistening in the full moonlight, which made the area as light as day. He looked into the courtyard where the young men and women of the house party were passing out into the lane in silent single file. Such was the custom on this the Twelfth Night for the purpose of gaining a knowledge of their destiny in what they regarded as the most important of events – marriage and death.

So much did they desire to see into their future that they would often practise the oddest of rites as you will come across in this book. Can you imagine these young people walking in single file across the snow covered fields, their intention to gather ivy leaves and bulrushes? With the aid of fire and water they thought to discover who in the next year was to marry and who was to die.

The old man gazed from the north wing window upon this tranquil view dreaming of his past.

The young folks reached the outer gate of the lane, near which they would have found the plants required for their spell. All were silent and taking care not to look behind them, as this, or speaking, would spoil the charm.

The leader saw what appeared to be the sea coming over the moor before a driving fog. She ran shrieking to join her companions who had by now also seen the waves fast approaching, rolling, curling and breaking upon the heath.

The old man was startled by the young people returning in fright. Running on up to the house the young people had dared not look back in their terror. But nothing more was to be seen.

They slammed the door shut – the others' laughter ceased and their music stopped dead. This house, in only a few moments, was shrouded in thick fog. All was still as death about the place.

Then a noise was heard. Like the roaring and moaning of the sea in a storm. The noise became louder and louder – as if

coming nearer and nearer. The crashing of the waves seemed to swirl around the house, almost as if the sea was breaking and surging right up against the house itself. In the wailing wind was heard the sound of oars rattling in their rowlocks and, for an instant, they heard the sound of oars being cast

hastily into a boat. Voices were heard. Smugglers past –
drowned with the old squire. Hailing their own names as
drowning men are said to do when they want assistance of
the living to procure them Rest.

All this time the green court appeared as if filled with the sea.
One could hear the breakers roaring as if on the cliff during a
storm. All the buildings and trees around the manor seemed
as if they had sunk into the ground. At length the surging of
waves and other sounds gradually died away, away, away…

The old man, observing all and having a clear conscience, feared
nothing evil in what appeared to him. He took it as an
unaccountable mystery – even in that time of marvels. Having
said his prayers he committed himself to the good Spirit's care.

Tired, he was more soothed than alarmed on hearing a
melody, until there was a change in the harmonious strains
growing more and more distinct. He heard these words
  "𝖂illiam 𝖕enrose arise.
  𝖆rise and avenge the murder of thy cousin's son".

Casting a glance towards the window from which the sound
had come, he saw an apparition of a handsome boy in a
shroud of white. The light which surrounded this lad
showed the likeness to be that of the lost heir of Penrose.

At this moment the room filled with the fragrance of sweet
springtime flowers. The old man, whom by now we have
guessed is William Penrose, spoke to the spirit and *conjured it*
to speak and to say what he should do.

*(according to the
form prescribed by
the Holy Church)*

(Jan/John)

Coming near, the apparition told how he had been murdered
by the pirate captain of the squire Jan Penrose on that grand
hunting day, and how his uncle had given the pirate a great
quantity of gold to do the bloody deed. Also that he had been
buried in the orchard under a particular apple tree – one that
would be known to William. This voice went on to say:
  "𝕿he murderer is now in 𝖕lymouth,
  keeping a public house, the situation of which…"

It then clearly described the location, finishing with –
"𝕎illiam 𝔓enrose, you will not have any difficulty finding it."

Then he could bring the murderer to justice by means of such
proof of his crime as could be found beneath the windblown
apple tree. Moreover it told William that the Spirits knew
that he had gone on a pilgrimage for their repose and that
they all, through him, sought his aid to enable them to rest in
peace. William promised to perform all according to the
wishes of the departed. Music was again heard and the
apparition gradually disappeared into the cloak of the night.

What William finds the next day…

The very weary man now fell into a deep sleep, awaking only at
the break of day & remembering that the late 'squire' had said:
> "Beneath the tapestry you will find a secret cabinet in which there
> is preserved a good store of gold and jewels for an infant heir.
> The key of this hidden treasury is behind the leaf of carved
> foliage which ornaments the bed head. You are to take the
> money for the journey and to keep the key."

True to his dream, everything was as he had been told.

Jan Penrose had often searched for this private recess, where
heirlooms and valuables were concealed. This would only be
known to a trusted guardian, or the heir – when of age.

The pilgrim now asked the old steward to accompany him a
little way on his journey. Before they parted the old steward
was to discover that he was actually in the company of   *(cousin to the squire*
William Penrose. In fact this was the very man who had left   *and the late squire)*
Penrose Manor so many years ago without trace!

The old steward told him of the noises and appearances which
had become so frequent of late – to the terror of all the
household. Then it was William's turn to tell of the night's
adventure and of the journey he had been exhorted to make.

...in Plymouth

Having reached the ancient place of Plymouth, William entered the bar of that mean public house to which he had been directed by the apparition. He found the former pirate captain lying stretched out by the fireside in a squalid room. From his demeanour he looked like a deserter from the churchyard – with his lurid glance and sunken eyes. William approached him with conversation about the West Country – of Sennen and of Penrose Manor – at the sound of which the ex-pirate captain begged:
"Mercy!"

He continued... confessing that he had been driven to the murder both by an evil jealousy that made him dislike the child and also by an unrequited love for the mother. It was for this, more than from any love of gold given by Jan Penrose, that he did do the dreadful deed.

William pondered on this hatred.

So, the pirate captain was from St. Just

The pirate captain continued...
"I am the wandering son – long supposed dead – of an ancient, respectable, but poor family whose ancestral SEAT is but a few miles from Penrose. Almost from childhood I have long and truly loved her and had my love returned, as I thought. Even then, that squire Penrose was advancing on my lady. In order to win the favour of my lady's parents, I left my home in St. Just on a desperate privateering expedition in the hope of soon gaining sufficient riches to win the family over."

SEAT – *home*

But before he could return with enough gold to buy the parish, Penrose had already wooed and won that lady – this pirate captain's first and only love. *Some* reward for all the suffering and hardship!

"With some of my wealth I bought a fast sailing craft – which passed
for a merchantman, privateer, or pirate. She was all of those during
the next few years as we roamed the high seas.
My crew were a desperate gang, loyal old comrades, who would
do anything to please me."
  "More through hate than love I planned to carry off the
  old squire's wife to a foreign land. Some while later,
  after a night landing in Whitesand Bay, me and my
  well-armed crew made our way to Penrose Manor."

But there he soon learnt that the love of his
life had been laid in her grave only a few days before.

After this he wandered over land and sea – caring nothing for
what became of him. One day he found himself cast upon the
Gwenver sands after his ship had foundered in deep water.
All but himself were drowned. He then worked for
Jan Penrose, as an earlier story told us. This culminated with
his murder of the uncle's child – paid for both in the uncle's
bloody gold and also by his own jealous driving hatred.

He had scarcely finished his sad tale when William Penrose
realised himself to be an old playmate of this wretched
man's innocent youth. William had only just enough time to
beg the pirate captain to give in ALMS of his ill-gotten gains,
when the pirate captain did draw his last breath.

ALMS – *these are*
charitable donations

The return to the West

Now William Penrose returned to the estate of Penrose and
made himself known – to the great joy of the old servants. He
found squire Jan Penrose gloomy, morose and ill-tempered –
who frequently wandered the hills, cliffs and other solitary
places for days and nights at a time. No one loved, feared or
even cared what should happen to this surly man. He was
absent when William, the steward, and other trusted servants
reinterred the child's remains from beneath the old apple tree
at Penrose manor over to Sennen churchyard.

Jan Penrose was no more seen alive in the old manor. The very same night that the remains of the child were buried in consecrated ground, he was found hung in the room of the apple tree plaster cast frieze. It is thought the frieze was placed in memory of the child and remains there to this day.

Following the spirit's compelling instructions he had still to find and remove the bodies of the old squire and his crew.

SANDED — *stuck fast on the ebb tide*

It was supposed that they were SANDED near Gwenver. Ghostly lights had been seen, sailors had been heard calling their own names. Folk lore has it that the drowned sailors did this to help in the discovery of their dead bodies.

old picture showing Chapel Idne to the lower right and also The Tribbens channel at low tide — see later

Next day these bodies were found at the spot where fishermen had heard the *calling of the dead*. As they'd all a great love of the sea, their remains were laid to rest with all holy rites in an ancient burial ground near Chapel Idne. The wind and the waves here would sing an everlasting requiem in their beloved music — the swirling of the sea.

William, now heir-at-law of the BARTONS of Penrose, Brew, Bosfranken and some other farms in the West Country, gave up his rights in favour of another branch of the family. He, disliking to live in the place connected with melancholy events so close to his heart, resumed his travels and was supposed to have died in the Holy Land.

BARTONS —
farmyards

The Penrose's in the West are said to be descended from this family, with whom the Pendrea's (Pendar's) are intermarried.

Old Justice Jones & the Vingoes of Trevilley

Old Justice Jones, who one time resided at Penrose Manor, was unquestionably a tyrant who took advantage of his office as a man of the Judiciary. Many men in the parish — even farmers themselves — did the work on his farms at Penrose and Brew for little or no payment. This on the worthless promise that their sons would not be impressed to SERVE THE KING. Magistrates were entrusted with warrants which empowered them to draft whomsoever they pleased. Therefore he had only to imply you'd be press-ganged into the Service to force an issue! This gave him scope to have work done for little, if any, return. He compelled all the labouring class to go to church every Sunday. In a case of non-attendance he had the right of law to levy a fine or even enforce imprisonment.

SERVE THE KING —
drafted & sent to crew
a man-of-war

Justice Jones would be first to leave the church (I suggest it would have been St. Buryan Church) but would wait in the churchyard to give his command to whomever, for the work he needed done during the week. During a harvest people would be required in a great hurry. He would then hoist a flag up his flagstaff. This used to be placed in a large holed stone purpose-built into the top of the angle formed by the green court and garden wall at Penrose. The granite base is still there.

Of anyone not receiving sufficient wages it was said to be like *Old Jones's Payment* or like a kick in the rear. Many men had to neglect their own harvest work to save that of Jones's. It is to be remembered that much work was done by hand and not with the drying facilities as we have today. All of which made farmers so much more conscious of the importance of the weather and of the time available to save such crops.

Trevilley – a small area near Land's End

The Vingoes of Trevilley were among the poor folk of those days, though this was an ancient Norman family who had held Trevilley ever since the Conquest. It is said they were the wine tasters to Norman chiefs. The Vingoes regarded Jones as nothing but an upstart stranger in the West and were prominent in doing all they could to check Jones's predations.

Morvah is near St. Just – Priest Cove is near Pendeen

One day a smuggling crew came to their aid. The crew just happened to be made up of local lads and farmers' sons – some from Morvah. Also a 'Daniel' and 'Ustick' believed to be related to the Vingoes, who were styled as gentlemen conveniently located at Priest Cove.

BASTINADO – *a beating on the soles of the feet*

On a fine day, when Jones had summoned all to do his harvest, that band of men took the law into their own hands and, taking up arms, marched down to Penrose Manor. They took Jones and his main manservant, a rogue equal to that of Jones himself, from the house. Hanging both these men head down off a tree in the yard they gave them a BASTINADO until they were within an inch of giving up the ghost. The two old sinners were made to give money to treat them to a jovial day, one and all, at the *First & Last Inn* [which is still trading]. Before leaving Penrose they told Jones that, if he ever attempted to return to his old tricks again, they would come some fine morning when he least expected and take him off to his cousin *Davy* Jones's Locker! From that time on he had such a fear of the men he seldom left his den.

In and around Penrose Manor

Families who have lived at Penrose Manor down through the centuries, even to the present day, have remarked on various ghostly experiences. In almost all cases they have not been frightened by the experience or of its presence.

The overmantle is still at Penrose Manor today, sculptured out of a single piece of granite and painted in, what is understood to be, the true and original colours.

the overmantle is illustrated on page 46

In Saxon times it is thought that every parish had a priory or monastery – for Sennen it is thought to be here at Penrose Manor. The style in which the house is built certainly lends one's mind to the idea. With low ceilings, extra wide doors, little back courtyard, windows all around you, you have a secure feeling... yet the feeling someone is peeping at you. I imagine this little courtyard must have been a beehive of activity in its heyday.

the river – bubbling through to Penberth

This little Penberth River runs on through Penrose and Bottoms, flowing into the sea at the picturesque Penberth Cove.

I assure you that the view, from within the house of the surrounding country, is something one never forgets. Very different from what we

Penrose situation:
Ordnance Survey
ref: SW 377255

have come across on our journey. The way these rolling hills
meet – one within another – is just amazing. The sun throws
shadows which exaggerate the steep inclines which run down to
a very special point at the foot of the Penberth River valley.
This is the point at which our three parishes St. Buryan,
St. Levan and Sennen meet. Here you touch all three at once!
The OS map reference is SW 380253.

From Henderson's book [5] we learn:
> "The house is built where a line drawn from St. Just to St. Levan
> Churches crosses another drawn from [St.] Sennen to St. Buryan."

Here also was the situation of the Penrose Mill.

In the survey dated 1778 the fields nearby were called
Great Clapper, *South Clapper* and *Little Clapper*. Another field, which
looks across into the house and is called *Oxon Downs* or
possibly *Ceely Downs*, Mrs. Sparrow [of Lamorna] believes to be
the site of an encampment for 100 men during the Civil War.

Referring to Coate's "Civil War in Cornwall" [6], Francis Jones
was a Royalist like his Basset step-relations. Listed in the
Protestation Returns as Francis Jones, Esq. 1641.

There is a mention of a Captain [Francis] Jones fined for his
Royalist activities in 1649 the sum of £222-5s-0d.
Also named as one of those who met at Trerice in 1655 to
arrange another rising – which never took place.

*Trerice is near
Summercourt*

In the upper room of the north wing there is a plaster work
TYMPANUM of an apple tree with narrow frieze below.
I've been given to understand that this type of gable end
plastering was typically early Elizabethan. Dr. Geoffrey Beard
saw a photograph and said he did not know of any example
later than 1560, although he did not rule out the possibility.

TYMPANUM – *an
ornate recess above
the doorway lintel*

Some ownership details of Penrose

1303   Records show a Penrose family. Thought to have
        stayed in occupation until about the 1550's.

1600   [approximately] from Magna Britannia [7] ...

    "The defeat of the Spanish Armade did not protect
West Cornwall from raids from Spanish galleys, most of
the barques in West Cornwall had been taken by the
Spaniards. They were succeeded by the Barbary pirates
who also raided the coast unchallenged. 1625, over ten
days, they took 27 Cornish ships & 200 men, as well as
60 men, women and children from a church in
Mount's Bay. The loss of ships was the ruin of the
Penrose family of Sennen."

A mortgage [date unknown] variously described to John Connock & Peter Marke (both of Liskeard) and to John Connock who died 1581. Possibly Peter Marke took over the mortgage and foreclosed.

Ralph Penrose had already sold outlying property, part of the manor of Lanyon, to John Rashleigh of Fowey in 1578.

Trust deed [dated 1553] in which Joseph Penrose named Ralph Penrose, John Treuryn and William Lanyon as trustees for his considerable property in the manor of Lanyon with the reservation that Penrose be held for the use of his son and heir Benedict Penrose and Joan Lanyon, whom he was to marry, and their issue. The rest to go to Joseph Penrose's *right heirs*, whomever they might have been. In fact Benedict inherited everything, possibly corroborating the legend of the murdered heir — reputedly buried surreptitiously under an apple tree in the orchard [the apple tree died 1983]. It has also been said the lad was murdered in the room with the plaster of the apple tree and that the uncle, who arranged this deed, hung himself there. Note that this appears to contradict detail in Taylor's [8] book where the malt house was so specified.

orchard — the right meadow, on entering the Penrose farm lane & just before crossing over the little stream

Benedict and Joan Penrose's son Ralph is presumed to be the mortgagor.

Francis Jones was established at Penrose by 1616 — as purchased from Peter Marke.

I write here from the notes kindly given to me by Mrs Hosking of Penrose:

see also Jones ancestry — Appendix pages 158-9

> *Jones ownership...*
> *Francis Jones bought Penrose from Peter Marke; the son of Hugh Jones who married as his second wife Jacquet Basset (widow of George Basset of Tehidy) and of Joan Lambe of Colston, Wiltshire; he also married Elizabeth daughter of Sir John Lambe of Colston.*

1872   Penrose became the property of Viscount Falmouth.

Here seems a good spot to introduce to you the granite overmantle depicting the Jones's arms.

The left portion's heraldic description is…

> "*Checky* of *argent* and *or*; on a *fesse gules*;
> three leopards' heads *proper*, each
> surmounted by a *fleur-de-lis argent*."

I believe she has found the answer to these arms to be that of the family known as the Lambe's [sometimes Lamb's] of Wiltshire with its coat of arms.

The official heraldic explanation is…

> *Sa on a fess or, betw. three cinquefoils erm.*
> *Two mullets of the field crest,*
> *on a mount vert a lambe or.*

My interpretation is…
> Black on a band of gold,
> between three plants of
> five leaves ermine spotted.
> Two stars of the field ridged,
> on a mount of green
> a mantling gold.

The centre portion bears the date 1668.

It is Mrs. Sparrow I thank,
for her endeavours in searching for the truth.

checky/squares
argent/silver
or/gold
fesse/band
gules/red
proper/natural
colouring
fleur-de-lis/triple
petalled flower

Strange Trevear

After leaving Penrose Manor [farm house] with its long narrow lane you travel through a strange barren track that is the valley of Trevear. Here is a spot one feels could be from another country — Spain or maybe South America, even a cactus plant would not be amiss. It is but a short track but in Cornwall your imagination can run wild in such a spot as this. No wonder the poets, the writers and the artists of this world flock to our county for inspiration, or to pass life at a more leisurely pace.

Seaward to Sennen

Going seaward

continuing carefully on this narrow, twisting and quite undulating country lane towards Sennen

Going towards Sennen — which is not far *over the hill*. The reference to 'over the hill' and 'under the hill' used to relate to the people of Mayon — over the hill — and the people of the Cove — under the hill. Those in each community considered each other as a separate group of Sennen persons!

turn left at the A30 (at the junction is an old milestone dated 1837)

Now we have the ever changing view of the sea to our right and, to our left, we will pass the school that's not long celebrated its centenary.

The *Magna Britannia* [7] has Mayon as the principal village and post town of the area. In earlier times it must have been at the hub of all business and the exchange of news. Others mentioned:

Sennen area
St. Levan area
ditto
St. Buryan area

> *Penrose and Trevear (I would have thought Trebeheor).*
> *Bosistow, Raughton [commonly called Raftra], Trevean, Trengothal and Treryn [Treen].*
> *Tregurno, Selena and Als of Alfa [now spelt Alsia].*

47

The Mayon part of Sennen

Here there is much activity – with its craft shop, Fish & Chip shop, Post Office, garage, a village shop with a remarkable range of supplies, meadery, guest houses and just a few private dwellings – all within a very small area.

This is also the place to ask the whereabouts of the stone known as *Table Maen*. Its size is some 6 – 8ft in irregular circumference and about 4ft high. It has been said to have been brought in by fishermen, after it was caught up in their nets, from beneath the sea where the land of LYONESSE lays.

King Arthur and his Knights are said to have dined on it after defeating the Norsemen – in a battle that was so bloody that a mill was worked with the flowing of Danish blood.
[previously referenced in the account of Trembothick]

The Table is also connected with stories of Merlin the Prophet. He forecast that the end of the world was near. So serious was his forecast taken, it has been said, three Kings sat there to discuss the situation:
King Athlestan, King John and King Stephen.

It came into further use for Perkin Warbeck (The Pretender) in 1497, after he landed in Sennen Cove during the reign of Henry VII. He went on to raise an army to march on Exeter.

In fact King John (who reigned 1199 to 1216) also landed at Sennen, on his return from his conquest of Ireland.

(LYONESSE *is the fabled land, betwixt the mainland and the Isles of Scilly, that is said to have sunk at an alarming rate one night; it had some 140 churches whose bells, sailors are said to have heard, peeling through the waves* ...*even today!*)

Table Maen shown from an old postcard (is situated on left side of road but in a built-up area)

To Sennen Church

(outside wall)

There is a dated stone [520 A.D.] in the boundary wall which shelters the building a little from the winter gales.

church is on the left side of the road with a car park to the rear

Right away, from its tiny door in, you'll not fail to be impressed by Sennen Church's cleanliness and orderliness. A reflection of the pride of the people in charge of our last church this side of America. Its brass adornments of course makes the quiet sparkle of this little haven of peace even more exaggerated when the electric lights are on.

I am told the choir pews were designed by *Wheatly of Truro* in 1939. They show angels singing – with some playing musical instruments. I feel sure that the date ought to have been much older but have been assured that is not the case.

At the back of the altar there are some scenes, which were worked as late as the 1950's, of the life of the people of Sennen. The pulpit is dated 1929 with very full and fine detail which I would have associated with an earlier period. These carvings are of St. John the Baptist, St. Sennen and the patron saint of sailors St. Nicholas, along with such details of shellfish, seahorses and seaweed.

There are a number of headless figurines. One is of the Virgin and Child and was restored by Mrs. Sheila Cavell Hicks (formally of Tregiffian). It was found in the wall during the eighteenth century [dated C] and thought to have been hidden in the wall during pre-Reformation times.

To the right of the east window is a faded mural. This one was uncovered in 1867 together with others in the transept which had gone beyond hope of preservation. It is said to depict The New Jerusalem, as described in Rev: XXI
> *...three embattled towers, from which streamers are flying,*
> *on a bridge with water flowing beneath...*

About the year 1430 A.D. parishioners of Sennen are said to have petitioned the Pope *all the way off in Rome itself* for permission to bury their dead at Sennen. It appears they had to carry them to the village of St. Buryan — some three miles away.

"As our village lies on the sea shore, we cannot accompany our dead all the way to St. Buryan — lest our houses be raided by pirates and enemies in our absence."

A very fair statement and testament to the times in which they lived. Remember, much of their journey would have been on rough tracks and they would have been away a long while from home. With most of the people being related in this close knit community, it meant only a few of the older persons and some of the very young would be likely to be left behind. Therefore the whole village could have been quite void of any able body should an emergency have occurred.

The Dean [Fitzeroy Henry Richard Stanhope] got his position to this area, it seems, through a shortage of bestowable titles after the battle of Waterloo! The Duke of York pensioned him off with the Deanery of St. Buryan. This included an income from both St. Levan and Sennen of £1,000 per annum for some 47 years; yet he is believed never even to have walked on the soil from which he derived so much income. He is said to have paid his curates three some £100 each per annum. It is, I think, possible that our Rev. Spry was one of these curates, for he is recorded to have been the Curate from 1816–1826.

Parishioners liked the Rev. Spry for his cheerfulness and also that he'd never weary them too deeply with religious conviction. They would neither complain if he was early or late, nor indeed if he didn't turn up in bad weather. It is reported that this could have been sometimes weeks at a time during the winter. His little dog, called *Sport*, was never far.

Refreshment time at the *First and Last*

a few yards further

This little Inn, with its exterior so little altered,
is easily recognised from old photographs.
It is just a stone's throw from the church.

Millions of people must have passed it by now, as everyone who walks, rides, or whatever to do the charity raising distance from John O'Groats to Land's End is sure to have passed its door by just a few yards.

Smuggler Joe

In 1805, at the First and Last Inn, a smuggling story is to be told connected with Joseph Pollard – a well known smuggler of the time. One of the cargos was said to come to some 1,000 gallons of brandy, the same of rum, also of GENEVA, of gin and other less valuable items.

GENEVA – *a spirit flavoured with juniper berries*

There was a violent affray when the Excise men arrived and seized the spoils. Joseph Pollard was charged with inciting the crowd – he also happened to be a part owner of the cargo! The chief witness for the Crown was one Anne George [a Landlady of the First and Last Inn in those days]. Indeed she was said to be a notorious informer. As to her whereabouts soon after this trial, this was 'unknown' and really no one seemed to care...

(retrace your steps back towards Pz; a little way before the Garage there is a pathway on the left leading seawards)

Now, down to the Cove

Let's find the footpath – it's to the left side of the Garage. It goes over several fields, straight over Maria's Lane and on down STONE CHAIR and into Sennen Cove - *under the hill.*

STONE CHAIR – *a passage to the Cove (steep in parts)*

Once down there, look over to the left (beyond the far car park) and you will see the coastal path to Land's End, with its granite cliffs where the weather has worn this hard stone into shapes both stark and whimsical. One such is named Dr. Syntax Head and he looks a bit of a *head-banger* to me. There is a small lookout room, a little way off and up the cliff, that gets well covered with sea spray when the sea changes its mood to one of anger. From one so calm, flowing as quiet as a river, it can change with the help of a whipping wind to a thunderous swirl in just a short time – making even quite large boats look like helpless punts.

seen safely from the seaward edge of the far car park

It is when the sea is in this mood, even more so on the Spring tides (I understand this to be governed by the moon and not the apparent season of the year!), that the breakwater in front of us looks like a giant waterfall with

water cascading over its full length. It is not always wise to walk out on it to the end, as you can see here. Often the foaming white maelstrom can be caught as glittering 'gold dust' by fleeting rays of sunshine.

Unfortunately this is the time when the lifeboat is most likely to be called out to assist any boat which might be in trouble hereabouts. The small cluster of rocks forming COWLOE would likely be completely covered when the tide is in such a rage. It is only when the Springs are fully out that one can fully appreciate the skills of the coxswains. Let it be realised some calls are at night, with a howling gale to aggravate the situation, as he navigates his craft through The Tribbens. On a Spring low tide, they would have to go around Cowloe. Only on a good high tide is it feasible to navigate through this passage. It's not that narrow really, the danger is from its very shallowness.

COWLOE – *one of the little rocky outcrops in Whitesand Bay*

THE TRIBBENS – *is illustrated back on page 39*

if you walked down Stone Chair that is!

Here at picturesque Sennen Cove, at which we have arrived as if by the back door, we now come upon an area where much remains of a very long time past – although some modernisation has taken place. For this moderation we must thank the District Councillors for their diligent attention to detail when building plans went before them.

Amongst the many very lovely cottages of an era long gone we come to the *Round House*. This is perhaps the first building you question. It sells good quality craft work but, for many years, it housed the SEINE. I understand there is nothing mysterious about the origin of it being round, other than it was the owners' preference to have a useful round house built over the

SEINE —
a large net

winch, which was operated by men to haul the boats up from the shoreline.

Then we come to the tall granite lifeboat house. This is worth another stop. Have a chat with the fishermen who are often to be seen here — see the lifeboat itself inside.

The fantastic endeavours of the men who go out to save life, by risking their own, are recorded within for all to see.

Winter storms were gnawing at the shoreline between the lifeboat house and the beach, so the esplanade was built recently. This makes for a more carefree walk for visitors and is a big relief for drivers.

The whole area is a place where you can let your imagination run riot into the past. Also where it's not difficult to visualise children at play, or adults working in the old ways.

The RNLI's 'Lifeboat Day'

A public relations day for the RNLI if you like – usually held in August. If you are in the cove on this day, do take a trip in this craft across the bay, sometimes around to Land's End. I assure you, it's an experience you'll find unforgettable. So is a walk along the breakwater – be it understood at your own risk! You will probably find people rod fishing on it almost any day of the year.

The Sennen seine

This is the bay where very large shoals of pilchard and mullet have been caught – even in recent years. In the past, fishing here was on such a scale that the whole cove, indeed the area about, must have got its living indirectly through it. Gone are the days when easy *treasures* could be hauled out of the bay.

HUER – *cliff top watcher & director*

Once the HUER raised the alarm telling the cove that a shoal of fish was amassing, all women and children would be ordered indoors. This for fear the shrillness of their voices would scare the fish away. Visitors were indeed *not* encouraged.

I've lived all my life just two and a half miles from the seine and the excitement has always been over before I've known anything about it. I would have so much liked to have witnessed the building up on the excitement, even the fraying of tempers, as the shadow of the fish swam to and fro.

When the right time was reached, and the huer sometimes waited for weeks, the signal he'd make.

Across the bay the first boat, called the *slip-net*, would quietly and gently let the quarter mile long seine into the sea. The obviously named second boat, the *follower*, proceeded to bring the net in a circle and to hold the ends together. The seven foot deep net was floated by corks and stiffened by grappling irons on the bottom. A third boat, called the *lurker*,

would be let into this vast mass of fish to scoop out a more manageable quantity, using the *tuck net*, for transfer to shore. It is recorded to have taken up to 17 or 18 people to work these three boats. For a catch of mullet, as the seine got lighter, it would be drawn onto the shore.

*Sennen seine —
showing the area
Sunny Corner top
left & Vellandreath
top centre*

By now, as we can all imagine, the water's edge was in full contrast to the unnatural quietness of the previous days. We now have the noises of men, women and children – along with their horses, carts and the calls of the dogs. With so much movement and bustle the excitement must have been up to the extent of a crescendo.

*a pilchard haul at the
Sennen slipway*

Now all able-bodied persons were put to work in real earnest. The fish were carried by the women in SKIP and MAUN. Then up onto the carts of some local farmers, whom I suppose were in on a share – the same as the rest! Up the slipway and off into various places, to be gutted, cleaned and salted away. This work could go on for days.

The farmers didn't much like working their horses this hard with such heavy loads in these difficult conditions. It was not only tiring on the beach, but then the hard drag up on the unmade road and its very steep hill – even before the journey to market.

Trouble... from Par

About 30 years ago a shoal of mullet was the cause of a
disturbance at Sennen. Par fishermen thought to cash in on a
Sennen shoal, as there was a shortage of fish in their own
waters. The argument got to such a pitch that the police were
involved and they had to stop the men from Par at the top of
the hill. The turbulence was such that it got mentioned in
Parliament. It was eventually resolved by the men of Par
returning home.

(north Cornwall)

It was said that the Irishmen who were building the Drift
dam came quickly to the aid of the Sennen fishermen!

Trouble... at St. Levan

People of St. Levan tell of a time, many years ago, when a shoal almost swam into the Sennen seine but just turned around short. The men set to sea, following along the coastline, only to see them settle at Porthgwarra. Here the men of Porthgwarra and those of Sennen came to blows! In the end the Porthgwarra men won the day and, it is said, that it took them *three weeks* to move the shoal from their net in that small inlet. Each basket had to be carried over the cliff and along a narrow path before being dealt with. The catch was so big that, even after these three weeks, the net had to be released before all the contents were dealt with! It is thought that a storm threatened and there was a risk of losing the net.

unloading pilchards at Porthgwarra, near St. Levan

First the work...

This old photograph is of the most accessible slipway down
to the beach. It shows the cold, hard, tiring nature of the

work – perhaps even the stress, a word all too inappropriately
used nowadays. The money earned here was to pay for their
survival and indeed health through the winter. There was no
DSS or NHS to help out with wealth and health respectively!

*mullet catch on the
slip near Chapel Idne
(see also page 39)*

...then the pay out

This I found intriguing. A man of trust in the community
would be invited to a meeting of the [seine] shareholders,
which must have been someone from practically every
household. All would sit around the table. As you can
imagine, all these men were extremely knowledgeable of the
sea, but some were not so good at the division of cash. They
had the sense to call in someone who would adjudicate.

1. *All the money, in cash, would be in a pile at the centre of the table.*

2. *Each man would be given a coin of equivalent value.*

3. *The procedure would be repeated again and again.*

4. *When the coins couldn't be divided equally, they would then be spent buying sweets to be divided among the children.*

I'm told that nowadays the shoals of fish — be they pilchards, herring or mullet — come to the bay in ever decreasing numbers. Sometimes not at all. Previously the tales spoke of the shoals giving fishermen a fantastic financial return. There has always been secrecy and an almost jealous claim on any fish that would swim in the bay.

The seine today

At one time early this century a gentlemen recalled there being three cooperatives of some 50 men in each — all working from this cove. They also made work for rope makers, blacksmiths, boat builders, shipwrights, sail makers and twine spinners to name but a few.

But now only a few of the residents are of the fishing fraternity. So much so, just a few years ago, I'm told the now depleted number of shareholders decided on a *smaller* net! Even so, should a mass of fish come in and fearing the obvious, the fishermen knew they would need more hands. They asked other local men if they would like to buy a lifetime share in the new net at £200 a share. I understand that there were no takers, although they were prepared to be paid as helpers on those occasions.

As things turned out, they would have recovered their money on the first catch. As they say *'no risk — no have'*.

Salt workings?

The survey of *Domesday* mentions ten salt works. One is said to have been in the Sennen parish, but I haven't been able to establish this as yet.

Dr. Borlase spoke of seeing where remains of the salt works could be seen. He added that...

"according to the tradition of the place, the works were discontinued, not through any lack of material or incongruity of situation, but through the deficiency or dishonesty of the persons employed."

A walk along the beach

Sennen Cove has a lovely fine golden sanded beach that can be easily reached. I hope you'll not be clock watching while on this trail, as so much of your time can go just chatting to us locals or peering into the rock pools to espy the little soft-shelled crabs, the little silver fish, the many varieties of seaweed and fragile shells. The tide line abounds in delicate colours – even the pebbles and quartz are in unbelievable colours. This, even more so, under the clean clear sea water in the pools that form here and there among the rocks.

go away from the Round House & towards the beach

Along the golden sand, so gloriously fine – enough even to go into the now old fashioned egg timer. There are different shades of green given by the distinctive vegetation of the area contrasting against the silver grey of the granite rocks and also against the reflection of the sky in the sea with its blue, slate grey or many shades of green. The picture is ever changing. It's not at all difficult to understand why we're in no hurry to leave, and why so many families come back year after year.

now on to the beach or perhaps along one of several footpaths set into the dunes and cliffs

In fact I did not fully appreciate just what visitors got so excited about until I travelled to some of the country's other holiday spots, with their dull mud-like sand and the dead colours of the cliffs. But, there again, I could be a little biased!

Along the first section is a beach cafe and gift shop – set into the shallow cliff. Further on, the attempt to stabilise shifting sands with dune grass and posts appears to be succeeding.

Just past the lifeguard's hut, nearer to the cliff edge, there is a clump of sea holly. The first I'd ever seen was right here. It has the appearance of a low holly bush, with prickles just as sharp I can assure you. The soft shade of apple green is in strong contrast to the wiry dark green grasses upon which we walk. Similarly we notice the contrast of the round pillow-like mounds of sea pinks with spiky green leaves and pink blooms gaily waving in the wind.

sea pinks – armeria maritima

Further along the cove

the paths go slightly inland into the area known locally as Vellandreath, or you might just stay on the beach

What sights to behold! With an expanse of coastline trimmed with fine grained golden sand the eye is carried around to the farthest point of land. Past the nearer cliffs – areas known locally as *The Barges & Escalls Cliff* – around to that of Cape Cornwall which is one of only six such Capes in the world. You may find it easier to get to the Cape by driving via St. Just, than by walking along the cliff. The path can be difficult to negotiate for the very young or, alternatively, the not so agile.

I suppose it is possible to find, at any time of the year, flowers amongst the crevices framed by the lichen and moss covered rocks. May month onwards would be the best time of the year to see the full array of such flora.

An additional attraction is the setting of the sun. A long path of gold will shimmer from the horizon to the water's edge, as the sea gently wavers to and fro. When it slowly sinks below the horizon it will send its rays of golden red in a semi-circle over a vast area of the sky.

All this and more is to be seen as we tiptoe through the grass and over boulders of granite through to the heather. Go around the gorse [!], it flowers much of the year with a strong golden yellow.

May is also the month of young wild life e.g. foxes, rabbits and birds. This area being so scarcely populated, that is by the human race, makes it a bit of a sanctuary. The loud crying of the swerving and swooping seagulls should ever warn of their presence. They will always be alert to any of your food, even that not yet thrown away!

After bouncing along on the springy grass carpet, or maybe you've chosen the softness of the sand, you'll come to the end of Whitesand Bay's beach. Around here is where the surf riders are in a world of their own. They can be seen in action all the year around, looking like the seals, or porpoise, you may come across in some quiet inlet.

Safety First at Gwenver

When the tide is out, one may walk on the sand around this point to a much more secluded sandy beach, Gwenver. This type of escapade is not to be taken lightly as our tides can come in quite quickly. It may be wiser to follow the cliff path and not be one of the statistics that stretch our emergency services to their limit. Often happening when the holiday season is in full swing. At this time the lifeboats, ambulances and helicopters, in fact everyone concerned with the rescue services, are worked to their maximum capacity. Sometimes this is all through people not really thinking that critical one step just ahead.

we are now in the area to which the Penrose story refers; this small cove is that known locally as Gwenver

Now make your way up to the top of the cliffs. It's a *good walk*, you may need a rest! Have a gaze around. Just take in the view of a coast being lapped by an azure blue to crystal clear sea. Each breaking wave introduced with white lace to the powder fine sand of the bay.

At the top [depending on your route] you should be able to make out one of the highest points around here. That hill of Chapel Carn Brea will be our turning point when we head over to the south coast.

there are several routes; at the top go on to make your way through to a narrow metalled lane — this is called Sunny Corner Lane

In the cliffs hereabout there still remain some of the concrete constructions built for the *Home Guard* lookouts during World War II, their duty to warn King and country of anyone who'd dare invade us. My father, like any able working man who did not go to the war, did his duty guarding our coastline in similar places. This was after many hard hours of manual work on the land during the day. Remember, little mechanisation was yet onto the farm, it being in the very early days of the tractor.

Once at the top of the cliff

follow it towards Sennen & inland; at the A30, turn left & head for Penzance; if you left your vehicle at Mayon then turn right here and return

take the left turn signed to St. Just

From Gwenver our journey takes us along the narrow tarmac lane which leads us back to the A30 road. This residential area is delightfully called *Sunny Corner* and justly so. Our journey continues & takes us past the, oh so isolated, Wesleyan Chapel at Escalls — which does open for services. I am always reminded of the *Hush-Puppy* advertisement when approaching this building — the windows for its eyes — the door for its tongue.

A little further on is the [Quakers'] *Friends Burial Ground*. It's the only one in the area placed on a plot which is a no-man's land — that belonging to no parish. A low walled burial plot at the apex of the road junction has a plaque recording some 36 interments between the dates 1659 – 1789. It is understood these people had a hard life in the district, with locals stealing their cattle and such. On the other hand it is fair to say that the Quakers would not pay dues to any church – as is mentioned in the booklet available at Sennen Church.

St. Just

Further on, we come to the aerodrome from where they fly to the Isles of Scilly and other places. By continuing you'll reach the old mining town of St. Just. The Geevor tin mine recently closed but it still has an interesting museum. There are also signs to Cape Cornwall.

But wait, we would then be over our self-imposed parish boundaries, so it's back to Chapel Carn Brea.

The view from Chapel Carn Brea

*turn sharp right just
before the aerodrome;
continue uphill; there
is a car park on the
right at the brow*

*(aerodrome – in the
distance at the
centre of picture)*

By now you will be well aware of the hill – Chapel Carn Brea.
This is where we are heading. Up this fairly straight but
narrow lane which is locally known as *bound and a half*.
At the very brow of the hill is a car park.

The walk to the summit, which even the most fragile of
walkers should attempt, will reward with a real appreciation of
the whole area. On a clear day the beaches and other outlines
of the Isles of Scilly can be seen, but I shouldn't try too hard
to see – the saying goes:
  "If you can see the Isles of Scilly now,
    then it's going to rain tomorrow!"

This is a terrific spot to watch the aerodrome below with its
many light aircraft zooming around. The view and sheer
variety of colour is certain to keep you spellbound.

Visible too is LONGSHIPS – off Land's End – about one and a half miles from shore. The original lighthouse was built back in 1795.

LONGSHIPS – *the lighthouse; this is an earlier one*

The book *Watchers on the Longships* [9] by James F. Cobb speaks of a keeper who was not initially aware of the reason for some *horrible noises*. They were actually caused by the pent-up air in the cavern below, but he became so terrified that his hair turned white overnight. It also mentions of a little girl who was left in the lighthouse on her own after her father [the keeper] was kidnapped by wreckers – so that the lamp might not be lighted. That night, when her father had not returned, she tried standing on a chair to light the lamp. She could not reach. After much ado and daring to stand on the family Bible, she used an upturned basin and managed to light the lamp. Thus giving out the warning to seafarers of the nearby rocky coastline. What a plucky and dutiful little girl!

A problem became apparent in the rock strata, so the replacement was built nearby in 1873. Very shortly after it was finished, the original rock base split to reveal an old cavity which had created such noises – so often mentioned in the early stories. I believe the structure was elongated later to cope with the ravages of the sea.

Then in 1974 an area was constructed on the very top so that the Trinity House's helicopter could land to bring supplies and change over the keepers. More recently Longships, like so many of our lighthouses, was converted to automatic unmanned operations.

You'll get a view of the busy maritime life with all its floating business of little fishing vessels, of the Isles of Scilly Steamship Company's *Scillonian* and of the sea ferry which travels from Calais to Ireland.

This is the spot in March 1967 from where my new born son and I witnessed the bombing of the crude oil spewing from the wrecked supertanker *Torrey Canyon*. This was the first real time our population experienced the disastrous consequences of a major oil spill. The scientists had given us warnings, but we had not imagined the scale of damage from just one ship. It coated anywhere that the tide reached. Some small harbours were completely covered with this thick, heavily viscous, sludge.

The smell of the oil was taken inland. We live three miles off either coast and, when the tide was in, the sheer smell was... oh so very prevalent! I dread to think just what the aroma was like for those who lived right there in the coves. Many of us, who had holiday visitors staying, were dreading the oil marks on our floor coverings and bed linen that season. There was no need to fear; I found guests much more thoughtful over this. The beaches had large ball shaped pieces of the wretched stuff. Thousands of sea birds died, others were saved by the kind attention given by people like the devoted staff of the bird hospital at Mousehole.

this little oiled up guillemot was at the Sanctuary within the half an hour; treated & was released to the wild several weeks later

Carn Euny...

Gold Herring...

There are views of the churches of St. Buryan and Sennen, along with the many farms that do abound hereabouts. The land is still of small meadows and of fields – not more than 8 to 10 acres. This helps to cut the winds that sweep in from the sea and gives protection to both cattle and crops. Some ancient lanes can still be seen. It's interesting to ponder the *why's and the wherefore's* of the lanes that now lie unused.

Look towards the St. Buryan church. Then, to your left and a little nearer, is *Carn Euny*. This is a site of an Iron Age village which is well worth a visit but takes you up a very narrow lane and then by foot. So too on the left is *Gold Herring*. A place named as such I know not why, but in its grounds are oval fortified walls with the later addition of a medieval smelting house and a furnace. The people who lived there were of the Bronze Age. *Beaker people* as they are sometimes called. These were the folk who arrived from the continent with knowledge of metals and are thought to be the people who placed the stones at the site we know as the MERRY MAIDENS. Further around is the *Boscawen-un* circle which dates back to around 1700 B.C. It is one of the places where Celtic Bards meet for the GORSEDD ceremony.

(MERRY MAIDENS
— more written later)

Boscawen-un...
...ask locally
for directions

The Gorsedd

At the Gorsedd, hundreds of people meet at historic open air sites such as this on the first Saturday in September. Though I recall one

GORSEDD — *sounds*
like Gore-Seth; spelled
Gorsedd (Welsh) or
Goresett (Cornish)

The Lady of Cornwall

from the car park, continue downward

such meeting held unusually in the St. John's Hall – because of such atrocious weather. On a fine day the spectacle is a memorable occasion out on the soft green grass and open granite. The *Grand Bard* leads the others all dressed in sky blue hooded robes. The hoods are worn by established Bards. The new Bards may only carry their hoods. The Grand Bard will blow a horn to all four points of the compass and a harp is played. The *Lady of Cornwall* goes forward carrying her *Fruits of the Earth*. Two page boys carry her long train. They are joined by young girls dressed in sage green with sprigs of heather attached. Speeches are made and prayers offered. Sometimes a new Bard is asked to respond with something appropriate to reflect the bestowed honour.

Crows-an-wra

CROWS-AN-WRA –
"cross of the witch"

GORD – *I understood this to measure around 9ft long by 4½ft high*

We come to the hamlet of CROWS-AN-WRA. It has been said the witch was one who did not do anyone any good but, in her favour, she did no harm.

There is a cross standing in front of an old Methodist Chapel, which was converted into a dwelling in 1982. Mr. G. Ellis says that the wall around the chapel was built by a Mr. Roy Lugg of Escalls for the princely reward of £0-00-18d a GORD. Right in front of the chapel there used to be a deep pool in which some poor horse drowned. There is also a quite ornate milestone – reputed to be one of the best in the country [about 1000 A.D.].

The narrow lane leading down through to Rissick Farm is only the width of a cart track. Lush wild grasses and flowers grow on either side of this lane, gently wavering to and fro as your feet brush past. I imagine it to be sheltered from most winds at all times of the year.

This little lane divides off several ways. There used to be a number of small farmsteads. Now they are the homes of people of non agricultural livelihoods. Some are holiday lets but thankfully some still have a few farming families who have lived in this vale for generations.

Further on, the lane divides into four directions: Boscarn Vean, Noonzarra, Rospannel & the ancient farmhouse of Rissick [Rissick appears in history books]. Besides this farmhouse being so very old, its other reason to be mentioned is that it was the first of six mills following the stream.

From springs around Rissick this little stream floats so quietly by your side, as it meanders at increasing speed through Rospannel, Alsia and Crean. At Tresidder it joins up with Penberth River before running out into the sea at Penberth.

straight across this busy A30 road (awkward in traffic – very much more so when returning)

continue down the lane to the bottom

at old Rissick, look back & outlined on a brow half-right is Boscarn Vean Farm (NightRider story)

the little stream runs underneath this bridge at old Rissick

The NightRider story

Our story begins at a homestead one quiet evening at
Boscarn Vean when dusk had truly fallen. The son of the
household decided to drive his car to St. Buryan. On leaving
the house he mentioned to his mother of the night's calmness,
such is the case when a swirling mist floats in – as if by magic.

He had gone but a short time, when a noise was heard at the
door. She thought it to be her son, being so soon after his
departure. Perhaps he'd forgotten something?

To her surprise it was a friend of the family standing before
her, white as a sheet, and in a state of shock. It was
surprising, as this particular young lady was not easily
frightened. Mother led her to a chair and this tale emerged.

As she was walking from Banns towards Boscarn Vean,
via No Man's Land, through the mist in front of her there
appeared the outline of a rider on a horse galloping at great
speed. As they pounded past her she realised there was no
sound. What's more – no head did the rider appear to have!
As for colours, well it was dark, so she just recalled the
general outline. Once past her the horseman made up the
lane towards Boscarn Farm [sometimes spelled Boscarne].

No ghost had been recorded in their valley. But they, being
of Cornish blood, did not deny outright the young lady's
story. They had known her for some years and she was not
one to take fright easily. They turned to talk of calmer
matters by their fireside.

Later that evening, when the son returned home, her tale was
confirmed by what he had to relate:

He was driving towards Crow-an-wra and had almost got to the
entrance of Boscarn Farm lane. Suddenly a horse and rider
charged out of the lane, galloped on ahead of him, turned into

Trevore Farm lane and disappeared into the mist.
With a jolt he realised the horseman appeared headless!
Later it occurred to him that maybe the horseman's collar had
been turned up, making the apparition just appear headless.

So this phantom was really seen twice in the same evening –
by two people – quite independently of each other.

Now the father felt he would like to experience this magical
mystery and often went into the fields there about, on such
misty nights as when that ghost was seen, but all to no avail.

One night some year or two later, in weather again of a quiet night with a swirling mist, the young people drove home from an evening out. The son got out of the car at the lower end of Boscarn Vean lane – to avoid playing *gooseberry*. The daughter of the household was taken up the lane. On returning to the end of the lane, the boyfriend driver was amazed to see the waiting lad still sitting in the hedge. He was shaking and white with shock – white as the Christmas rose and frozen to the spot. Some while later he revealed of seeing that same fine horse and rider as he had seen before. This time they passed by him at great speed from the Noonzarra land and on up the valley. Yet again no noise did the horse make and the dark misty outline of them both was remembered.

...who is the rider?

...who still rides in great haste?

...shall we ever know?

While trying to establish if others in the area had seen this ghost a somewhat amusing story emerged – with a sad ending. Our farmer, who still lives in the lane, recalled this of an evening after attending the St. Buryan Young Farmers Club. He was cycling home on the track through Banns to Boscarn. At the brow of the hill he almost brushed into a large dark object. With the roughness of the track and only a cycle lamp, not at its best, he couldn't be certain but he thought that he had almost ridden into a horse. When he got home, his father couldn't think of anyone's horse that it might have been.

Next day the boy was told to fetch that horse from the field but, as you might guess, it was not there. Where was it? *Could it have been our NightRider?*

But no.

(retrace your way back up the lane to the A30; then turn right to Penzance – needs some care!)

A few days later they learnt that the horse had made its way back to the place, not to where it had been purchased as a two year old, but back to the place where it was born some twenty years prior [the other side of Lamorna]. Unhappily, the horse was brought back and it died about fortnight later.

Returning to St. Buryan

From Crows-an-wra to St. Buryan, where the road divides from the A30, is the Trevorgans Cross. It has been moved to this more prominent site for its own safety from the end of Trevorgans Farm's lane near St. Buryan.

shortly – take the next right to St. Buryan (Trevorgans Cross is there on the junction)

Every year the farmers hereabout kindly give the committee for the *Western Area Agricultural Competitions* permission to use their farms. This means them arranging well in advance each year's crop. Fields will be needed for groups of classes from novice up to the expert. There will be the horsemen (though they are few now) and the finest of tractor pulled ploughs. But no doubts of which is the favourite to watch in action – of course the horse still gives the most pleasure.
A competitions marquee will be erected for the root crops, hay, silage, Young Farmers Clubs and any domestic entries with their preserves and cakes etc. Everyone entering will be eyeing the cups and hoping for it to be their lucky day!

the Western Area Agricultural Competitions 1992, held at Kerrow Farm by kind permission of W.H. Care & Sons

The village lane has been humourously called our *snowy mountain track* for, when snow does arrive – once every six years or so, the snow stays much longer here than elsewhere.

(Cecil Laity coming, Harry Kiff going)

St. Buryan Church – in more detail

*turn right at the church
& go on around into
the village's square*

Earlier in **Safari West** I wrote briefly on the formation of the St. Buryan Church, so here I include matters more recent.

May we now look at its furnishings.

As you enter the church, you get the feeling of an elegant House of the Lord – kept in fine repair. The replacement of old fabric with new is a continual process. Opposite is the door which is only used by a new Rector on *Induction*. The long solid wooden steps add to the feel of the occasion. Sometimes the steps are used as a focus in wedding floral decorations and harvest festivals.

The church has a very nice ℭ font. At three points there are angels supporting shields. The fourth has a plain cross and opposite a small Maltese cross. My twin, myself and all seven children were christened here at this quietly elegant St. Buryan font.

All the stained glass windows are of a very vivid colour and tell magnificent stories.

77

See here the ℭ tomb of Clarice La Femme Cheffrei de Bolleit, thought to be a mother of the farmlands of Boleigh which is near *The Pipers*. A large memorial on the back wall has a most intricately designed frame – in dedication to the Leis family of TREWOOFE.

TREWOOFE –
*sounds like Trove;
more of this later in
another story*

The soft furnishings are continually being updated. The embroidered KNEELERS, for instance, are an interest of mine and the many other members of the *Kneeler Class*. It's a labour of love. Generally our kneelers carry hidden stories and feelings. Some of the few I've embroidered:
> *Elephant, Horn of Plenty, Stained Glass,*
> *Sir Francis & the Cockerel that Crowed at Easter.*

KNEELERS –
soft prayer cushions

The pews are plain except for a few at the front.

Our choir wear a red and white surplice. St. Buryan Church is allowed to do so because of its Royal Charter.

The bell-ringers have been working hard and the tower can resound from the splendour of the world's heaviest *Peal of Six*!

It's a sad fact in our church's history that we have had some over-zealous *restorers* – spring cleaners more like! A catalogue of some of their actions includes:-

(1815) The ROOD SCREEN cut down, thrown into the tower. Singers' west gallery cut down, not a stick of the same retrieved.

ROOD SCREEN –
*the richly carved
wood screen; should
have a crucifix on
top but our's has
been lost*

(1886) Floors this time. All floor levels altered; those in the nave lowered and those in the chancel raised.

(1910) Belgian refugees returned parts of the screen [from storage in the tower] to the Lady Chapel. The original had a very rich and strong colouring. At one time the whole is said to have been painted red and blue with some gilding. The top section of the screen has a carved hunting scene with animals – symbolic of *Good reigning over Evil* I'm told. It also shows three crests.

The cross in the churchyard near the south porch is a Celtic cross, of workmanship thought to be from the ℭ but is set upon steps from the ℭ – a fine example.

Some years ago a young lady got off the Penzance bus – coming from Porthcurno with mainly school children on board. She was seen calmly getting off the bus and was wearing long flowing clothes – such as many artistic people choose. Then she wandered up the churchyard steps. Village life went on.

A fairly quiet time of day. People away at work. Children at school. Just a few village traders labouring. Such as those at the SMITHY, which used to be right behind the Post Office.

SMITHY – the blacksmith's shop

Suddenly the peace was broken with screams so horrific. The smithy brothers had no idea just what was happening. To their horror a human torch approached. Quickly they threw a horse rug over this walking flame. Not until they were told later did they know whether it was a man or a woman that they'd tried to rescue. Sadly this young lady lost her life. Apparently she had brought a can of fuel and matches so to carry out her self-immolation upon the steps of our ancient cross.

right outside the church's south gate

The other cross, of the ℭ, is built on a square base of granite. As a child I was told not to be seen climbing onto this square, as it was a burial chamber of a number of soldiers from a very early battle. Nowadays I can get not a single person to verify this. In fact they think this is *crackers* and otherwise suggest it being something to do with the village's market day Charter.

the village's Charter dates back to 1302

This little village square has seen many acts of turbulence and violence through the ages. Perhaps this spirit is what prompted

the film director Sam Peckinpah to film the '70s cult film
Straw Dogs right here in the village square. A rather more
serene affair was had during the '80s filming of *The Wesley Trail*.
In this film our very own Mr. J.M. Hosking [2] played a small
part. Many of both films' extras were villagers and other locals
– including me!

Of village trading and commerce

There are all sorts actually within St Buryan. There is a
carpenter, farrier, grocer, Post Office, Churchtown Farm
[eggs & cream], *Churchtown Technology* [my publisher],
hairdresser, plumber, builder, the St. Buryan Inn and a very
useful garage. Many small businesses trade and offer services
direct from their cottages; such as plumbing, gardening,
accountancy, decorators, arts & crafts, writers – the list goes
on… Of course most of the surrounding farms and
farmsteads have trading connections within the village.

*'Churchtown' is a
small area within
St. Buryan itself*

We have lost the man that served fish and chips, who also cut
hair and who mended our shoes. All that wouldn't be allowed
now with the Authorities would it? His prices were very
reasonable too. We've also lost the house with its resident
nurse; the house with its resident Primary School headmaster;
the policeman and his house; the smithy barn [now new
cottages]; the house with its resident butcher…
Things always change don't they?

The village hall

The village decided to form a committee to
revitalise our village hall for the more
general use of all the parishes around
St. Buryan. The Parish Church had long
played a worthy guardian.
There was a big Opening Ceremony…

...followed by a candlelight Medieval Banquet for some 100 guests in fancy dress.

Afterwards the committee set forth with many ideas. The first Christmas we painted colourful murals on the old limed walls. A later renovation removed that, oh so, damaging lime. The nice granite structure revealed was further enhanced with some fancy pointing.

the village hall is on the right a short walk, past the general store, down the road signed to Porthcurno

It all had to be done with little enough cash! Fortunately we were allocated some helpful grants to modernise and now take bookings from the old faithfuls (Male Voice Choir, Women's Institute & Young Farmers Club) and to the more recent groups and clubs such as mother and toddler sessions, indoor bowls and judo. Will we forget our very popular pantomime & drama group? *Oh no we won't!*

On the periphery of the village

leave the village square going down Rectory Road (to Lamorna); the school is to the right

Here is our Primary School – for children aged 5–11 years. The building is of fine dressed granite [dated 1910]. From here they can choose to join the Cape Cornwall (St. Just) or Mounts Bay (Heamoor) schools to continue their compulsory education. A previous school became our village hall.

slightly further on and to your left

The cemetery is used by both church and chapel. Some graves have rather fine headstones and verses. Once, the regular undertaker was taken ill just the night before a funeral. He told the Parish Council chairman that the grave was still not deep enough. So the chairman [then Mrs. Valerie Humphrys], rector and both spouses went to the cemetery come nightfall. While the women shone torches, the men dug deeper making sure the pit was large enough for the occupant next day. The funeral took place with the relations none the wiser, being spared any embarrassment and further anguish.

The playing field on the outskirts of the village hosts our cricket and football teams. There is a playing area for the young with swings, slides and a roundabout. On *Guy Fawkes* night the Playing Field committee used to organise a big bonfire & provide some fireworks. People were encouraged to bring more so as to add to the evening. In summer it hosts a Gala Week with daily organised events.

November 5th.

Opposite is the high well-built entrance of Lefra Farm. Mr. Prismus Jelbert, a very big fellow, farmed Lefra and built that lovely HEDGE to enclose the old St. Buryan Rectory.

a Cornish HEDGE
*is based on granite
and earth — not just
of trees & shrubs*

Confusion at Boskennal

Out along the road, quite level for a walker, we come to the farm of Boskennal. There used to be a misleading sign in the yard which pointed to *Penzance, St. Buryan & Sennen*. A lorry driver one day unloaded his part load here. He then opened the gate, as the sign showed to Sennen, got into the lorry and was about to negotiate the width of the gateway to deliver the rest of his load, when the farmer asked:
  "Where are you going to?"
Back came the reply:
  "Off to Sennen!"

*continue on out of
the village; past the
left & right zigzag;
on the next bend the
Boskennal access
lane is to the right*

It was then the farmer felt he should explain that the sign had been resited from the Boskenna Cross area when a new one had been erected. This particular one was only for decoration. A very red faced driver realised his folly. In no way should he have thought of crossing a *grass field* to go to Sennen! He smartly about turned his vehicle and drove back up the lane to the metalled Rectory Road.

*(unfortunately the
actual sign is no
longer at Boskennal
— seems like it is
destined to travel!)*

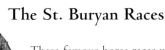

The St. Buryan Races

These famous horse races were run at Down's Barn Farm, which the Care family farmed. Racing reports even appeared in our local paper *The Cornishman* over a century ago.

About the year 1891, Mr. John Care was the man to ring the Buryan Bell that would start the Easter Monday St. Buryan Races.

In more modern times Mr. James Henry Care told me:

Down's Barn is the next farmstead on the right

Down's Barn race course was considered the finest race course in Cornwall. With its high but safe hedges you could stand on one particular hedge and see the race from beginning to end. Mr. Harold Thomas took a week to erect the lovely grandstand. He was a grandfather to the similarly named St. Buryan carpenter. [now retired]

I well remember one Easter Sunday morning looking up in the *Townfield*, where the grandstand stood, finding a man with his jockey and horse who had all come over from Ireland to try their luck the next day at the Races. My father told them to get out of the field [so as to favour our own home runners]. The Irishmen were staying the week at the St. Buryan Hotel, which was kept by Mr. George Hoskin from Trevorrian Farm [opposite Pridden]. Now he was also running a lovely mare called *Actress*. Apparently the Irishmen came here to beat *Lady Penzance* – a famous mare owned by Mr. John Rowe of Newbridge and ridden by his son Johnnie. She knew the course well, its hedges and the old *Lauis Lane* double jump. The Irishmen returned very disappointed!

We boys had the pony and cart to pick up any stones etc around the course. Later Mr. Prismus Jelbert would arrive with the soft cushioned *felts* which would go on the seats of the grandstand.

Mr. Robin Bolitho's groom, Mr. Charles Dale, would book up the loose box in our stable for his lovely pair of horses. Our workmen looked forward to Easter Monday, as they got many tips for looking after the horses – both in the stable and the cow shelters. To finish the day in style the committee would have a grand supper at the St. Buryan Hotel.

When my grandfather died at Boskenna he made my father promise to stop the Races being held at Down's Barn Farm. This was a great blow for the committee, but my father kept that promise. They never had a racecourse like it again.

James Henry finished up with:

My grandfather Henry Care was born in Towednack parish near St. Ives. The family of his brother John Care supplied the racecourse for the Towednack Horse Races. As a young man I went there, but it never had banks like those of Down's Barn.

I felt honoured on the 20th October 1985 by Mr. Oates when he came to Alsia Farm to present me with that starting bell. He asked that I keep the *Buryan Bell* safe and pass it on to a son in case the Buryan Races should ever start again. It had travelled to Wales with him but, at the age of 77 years, he thought it time to entrust it to someone younger. I find this a great privilege. The bell may have been a ship's bell & was found at Nanjizal [between Porthgwarra & Land's End].

on the bell there appear to be the engraved words:
Giuten Stockholm
1858
Joh A Beckman

Boskenna Cross

At the end of the lane we come upon Boskenna Cross;
a sculptured figure of a person with outstretched
hands instead of the more usual cross.

Tradition has it that a coffin was laid at the foot of this
cross while the bearers rested on their journey from
Lamorna to the St. Buryan Church.

Suddenly, a voice was heard from within and
therefore the journey was abandoned!
If you haven't already realised…
…the occupant was just not dead!

Tregiffian

*turn left to Lamorna;
at the bottom of the
slope is the Barrow*

*there is a glimpse of
the Merry Maidens
site on the next rise*

*sketch of the Barrow
find, about 8"*

Tregiffian is farmed by Mr. Derek Phillips. When I spoke to
his father, the late Mr. John Phillips and his mother
Mrs. Sarah Phillips, he told me that the farm was owned by
him and his father before. It has two historic Sites.

The first, at the start of the lane, is the Tregiffian Barrow.
This is a large burial chamber thought to date from 1900 B.C.
It was discovered during widening works of the B3315 road,
which will explain the road's odd deferment.
Miss D. Dudley was in charge of the necessarily hurried
excavation. Some few days after she had left, Mr. Phillips
thought he would like to investigate the inside of the Barrow.
With only his bare fingers, he succeeded in moving some soft
damp earth from around what looked like a bit of a pot. To
his delight and great excitement it soon became a whole pot.
Miss Dudley then sent him instructions on how to conduct
an emergency stabilisation [closely wrap in paper and leave to
dry out in an unheated room at a cool temperature].

The second historic site adjoins the field of the famous Merry Maidens. This site has fields called *Lower Tombis* [ref: 3470/1] and *Gabrias* [ref: 3433]. Here, stones may form another strange circle.

In 1948 a pottery beaker was found by Ms. Diana Shorpe [a potter] in what looked like a child's grave. It was given to the St. Buryan Church whose Rector [Crofts] was very interested in artifacts. Unfortunately it was later stolen from the church along with other interesting items which he had accumulated for the pleasure of parishioners and the many visitors.

sketch of the pottery beaker, about 5"

The Merry Maidens

Up in the adjoining field are the *Merry Maidens* or *Don Mine*. I've read that the people of the *Gold Herring* site might have placed these stones, which would date them from around the Bronze Age [1900 – 450BC].

just ahead, within sight of the Barrow

The more romantic tale is that on a lovely summer's Sunday the maidens of the village, while taking a walk along the cliff,

crossed the field on their way home. They heard two pipers
playing a delightful tune. Merrily they joined up, dancing in a
circle to the enchanting music.

All at once the sky darkened.

Thunder roared.

Lightning flashed…

…and the maidens turned into stone.

As the storm erupted the two pipers made off.

They too were caught at Boleigh Farm and turned to stone.

I remember that Gran would often tell me:

> "When the maidens hear
>   the bells of St. Buryan toll,
>   they will dance once again".

Took me years to work it out – stones can't hear… can they?

It would appear that the WWII story of the leading horse
inexplicably dropping dead and thus ending the ploughing
of the field is fanciful . The farmer then [Mr. Thomas] told
me that none of his horses had ever died that way!

The Pipers

BOLEIGH – *continue
past several bends; the
Pipers are to the left
before going down hill*

A more historically accurate tale of the Pipers [of BOLEIGH]
is connected with a battle. These two large standing stones
have sometimes been reported to form a site that marks
respect for the fallen men from an early battle.

The west field is called *Long Stone* field or *Gul Reeve* – possibly
a corruption of the Celtic *Gwel Ruth* meaning red. Strangely
there is no soil, stone or flora of this colour in the immediate
area. Historians have come to conclude therefore that this was
a site of a Bloody Battle.

Rumour has it that there are soldiers buried in a long trench
beneath the farmyard!

This is an area at which you will want to stop and ponder, in any weather – be it rain, mist or sunshine. Alive with mystery and intrigue. The panoramic view goes on for miles. When a mist envelops you, it is as if you have the whole world to yourself. Misty droplets form on the grass and hedgerows.

As the mist swirls away, a little here, a little there, glimpses of a distant farmhouse come into view. Far off villages and church towers can float magically above the ever changing scene.

A tale from Trewoofe

Gran used to tell me of a girl about nine years old and her younger brother who played for hours among the animals at TREWOOFE Farm – around the millpond, in the orchard and at the nearby Clapper Mill. Their father had gone on a crusade to a hot desert-like country in the Mediterranean. and their mother was very desirable. She capably managed the farms, all of the estate, organised their servants and still found time to be a caring mother. As comfort she and her nanny embroidered a life-size tapestry of her husband in his full battle regalia.

TREWOOFE –
*sounds like trove
(sometimes Trewoof)*

She was often harassed by a local landowner while her husband was away at the crusade. He was away so long it was commonly thought that he had been killed. This landowner thought he'd get rid of the children so that the mother, in her grief, would turn to him.

carry on downhill; note the right turn down to Lamorna, but continue slowly

One summer's evening the children could not be found. The servants, including the conniving landowner, searched the farms, woods and even the cave at the top of the hill. All to no avail. Tragically the children's bodies were found a few days later under the thick weeds of the millpond.

...just around the next right-hand bend turn left up into an unmarked lane; the millpond is right — where that lane sharply turns left

The wicked landowner had even joined in with the search thinking to improve his chances with the mother. Later he approached her in her bedroom. *A slight breeze made the bedroom door swing.* As it did so the tapestry gently moved. The landowner turned. For a split second he saw the husband had returned with flashing sword swinging. Panic-stricken, he turned and fled, bolting around the millpond. In his terror his heart stopped and he stumbled into the millpond. Thus he drowned at the very same spot where the wicked deed was done.

The children are said to have been heard playing around the millpond and up the lane to Trewoofe house.

Now go over *Oakhill* and down along for a short distance.
In early Spring this area comes alive with the bright hues of
the willow catkins. The *Lamorna Pottery* is a suitable place for
some refreshments & a browse through their delightful stock.
Alternatively we will shortly pass *The Wink* inn.

*return to main road,
turn left & continue
— the pottery is at
the next left junction*

While retracing your route, at the foot of Oakhill, you will be
able to see, on your left, the end view of Clapper ·Mill.

see Trewoofe story

Down in Lamorna

The valley

Into the wooded valley of Lamorna. These trees have been the
cause of much controversy in this particular valley. As you
will appreciate, this area has the greatest number of trees
that we have seen in the whole safari anywhere within
these last three western parishes of our Cornwall.
To keep this area replenished takes vigilance from
us all, especially to counter the otherwise
well-meaning actions of the *modern improvers*
who come to live among us and are intent in
tidying us up and in laying concrete.

*(retrace route to that
Lamorna junction
you noted earlier)*

A decade ago the ravages of the damage caused
by the dreaded Dutch elm beetle here, and at
Bottoms, was such that they became practically
devoid of trees. Look now at how nature has
replenished this area — with some assistance
from the landowners and concerned bodies.

We still have bushes in great profusion. It doesn't seem to have affected our summer dawn chorus of birds! Heard at full force from 4a.m. onwards. Take care not to miss this wonderful chorus by arising early... By 7a.m. they'll have disappeared, I know not where, for the rest of the day.

We go along these still and, now delightfully leafy, glades towards the cove. Stories of smugglers past, hidden here and there. Contraband under bridges. One smuggler hid himself with his *duty free* away from the hated Excise men. Rum and brandy appeared to be the sort of goods favoured by the locals. They weren't averse to fine silks which they could resell to richer, out of county, buyers. Also, as many spices were brought in from the Mediterranean, so it's no wonder we Cornish bothered little about England.

We pass homes of many a past and present artist and writer – even some quite famous ones. When you get here you'll know just what has drawn these people to such a place.

Lamorna

on your left

We pass the Lamorna Hall which was built as a school with the private income of Canon Coulson of the St. Buryan Rectory on land given by Mr. John Hosking of Boscarn. About 50 children attended. When numbers dwindled the children began to go to St. Buryan School. In 1965 the Church Council decided to sell the building to the local residents for the sum of £1,500, who then formed the committee that now runs it as a community centre and look how well kept it is.

looking left, down the narrow lane

At the strangely shaped crossroad, you can see the tiny Post Office which my great-grandfather Gartrell once ran. Every Sunday he walked the paths across the fields to Trendrennen Farm [St. Levan] to see his grandchildren, stopping off at Treen to get a *penny worth* of sweets. My aunt May, in her eighties when she told me, still remembered the general excitement on being told to line up in the farmhouse kitchen and to open her hands with her four brothers and three sisters. To each he would say:

"Oh, oh, what big hands you've got!"

Then, with a polite thank you, off the children would scamper.

Around past the tiny Post Office, we can wander to the mill whose wheel sometimes may be seen going round and round on its endless journey. It was carefully renovated in 1979 after some 40 years of silence. Mr. Hosking's daughter [Mrs. Fox] runs it as a little gift shop – along with the noise of ducks and peacocks as background.

Mr. Hosking was the last of the family to use the mill authentically

Retracing your way back from the mill you will see ahead the popular inn *The Wink* – after which you might walk or drive further on down the lane to its end at the cove itself.

mill's shop & car park are down the tiny lane past the PO

Lamorna Cove

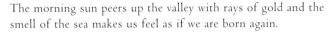

*the cove is found at
the end of the valley*

(DRESSED – *cut &
squared off edges,
sometimes also with
a decorative edge*)

The morning sun peers up the valley with rays of gold and the smell of the sea makes us feel as if we are born again.

Traditionally, on Good Fridays, hundreds of people have walked down the cliff paths from Mousehole and, like us, down this road. I'm not sure why this is – just that people do. As a young girl I walked here from Alsia with my sister Joyce. We looked out to sea, it seemed the right thing to do. There were many people milling about. No shops were open nor singing groups to draw us. There seemed an atmosphere as though something, I know not what, was to arrive. Nothing – so what was it that could have drawn us here?

Over to the left the cliff side granite quarry stands out boldly. This was worked in the latter half of the ⒸG. Large DRESSED granite blocks were moved out by chains down *Chain Lane* onto the boats. Looking at these massive blocks left in such disarray, it is beyond my comprehension how men could cut; transport to the boat; block and tackle into fairly shallow drafted vessels; reversed at end of the voyage; transported to the building site and finally positioned these monsters to plan.

Local destinations included places such as the Mousehole harbour wall, the base of the Sir Humphry Davy statue in Penzance and, of course, much was used at the St. John's Hall, Penzance. One of the Hall's steps is of a single solid piece of granite — over 17ft. long!

Further afield destinations included the River Thames' London Embankment and the now infamous *London Bridge* – designed by John Rennie [1831].

Later, London Bridge was sold for a sum in the region of $2½m and transported to the USA. This can now be seen at Lake Havasu City in Arizona. Water had to be diverted so as to flow under the 'bridge'. To help replicate a London scene they have a Public House nearby. Familiar red double-decker buses and large black London taxis also were brought in to drive over it. Both the *Union Jack* and the *Stars & Stripes* flags flutter in the desert breeze. Apparently there is even a recording of *Big Ben!*

the RNLI coming into Lamorna's little harbour on a Lifeboat day

The colour of this quarried granite is difficult to describe. Could it be silver, light beige, shades of grey or even gold with little diamonds, glinting as it does in the sunlight?

Once on the old harbour wall [built 1870] you will not fail to notice crystal clear water below, with the sunlight shimmering off the underwater granite boulders. Glimpses of fish, scales glistening, swimming to and fro undisturbed, like marine jewels winding in and out of the colourful seaweed.

Rising up on the path to the right, perhaps turn back to look down into this cute little cove which has much to thank Mr. J.J. Daniel who gave it a real good sympathetic face-lift before selling it to another Cornishman like himself [1983].

choose a suitable path, walk up out of Lamorna sufficiently to get a good view!

Shipwrecks

Even Lamorna can be stricken in storms, when the seas tear at the massive harbour stones like pebbles on the shore.

There was a very old wreck, the *Orient*, whose cargo of wood was used to make that cottage that continues its name. *'Waste not, want not'* is still very much our nature in these parts.

The *Avery* [possibly *Avebury*] had a cargo of hide and TALLOW. Its Captain was never found. His wife and two daughters aged 10 and 12 were placed in the *'dead house'* either side of their mother. They were said to have looked very beautiful.

TALLOW – *fatty substance used for making soap*

the wreck of the Conqueror near Mousehole

Not all ships are lost in storms. For instance the freezer trawler *Conqueror* was lost on the rocks near Penzer Point, which is further around towards Mousehole, in calm clear weather in late December 1977. I understand that too much trust was put in the autopilot, whilst crew was having breakfast.

The *Lady of the Isles* became grounded in 1904. Ironically she later became a salvage boat. In her heyday as a passenger carrying vessel she sailed between Penzance and the Isles of Scilly.

The *Solomon Browne*

Most people of this country will recall the sinking of the Penlee lifeboat off St. Loy during a ferocious storm on 18th December 1981. The crew braved this to go to the aid of the stricken *Union Star*. Despite the seas being so rough the mostly Mousehole crewed lifeboat went alongside the ship time and time again to rescue the cargo vessel's crew of eight, a woman and two children. We believe that, just as the final person was about to be rescued, somehow the lifeboat was cruelly struck against the wreck. Tragically those rescued were lost again – alongside all of our RNLI menfolk.

Being so near Christmas the tragedy touched hearts worldwide. A fund was started spontaneously and donations flooded into Mousehole from locals & visitors alike, wishing in some way to show their respect to men of such courage. Nearly £4m was raised and this time it went straight to the next of kin. A similar fund, set up after the St. Just Geevor Mine disaster, was blighted when some people of authority *tied it up* making it very difficult for the next of kin to benefit.

The replacement lifeboat is of the bigger and more powerful *Arun* class – so as to cope with such conditions more safely. The Penlee lifeboat station doesn't house its boat anymore. Too big to be ramp launched, the lifeboat is moored at Newlyn. Shortly after the disaster Mr. David Robinson offered a large amount of money to build the replacement boat – which was subsequently named MABEL ALICE. The new coxswain had to move from St. Buryan to be close to the boat's new moorings.

MABEL ALICE –
after his wife

My publisher purchased that coxswain's St. Buryan cottage, from which he now works…
…such circles!

96

Around Tater-du

describing a cliff top route is a bit of a problem; walkers are now on their own! ...we will meet you again at Penberth

Take a path to the west. Onward up this cliff. This will sort out those of us weak or feeble in a very short time. At the top the view is just so fantastic one could just stop and stare for an absolute age. Whether the weather be one of a calm sky and blue sea, or that of a tempestuously stormy black, the sheer gamut of visual elements will abide in your memory forever.

Hereabouts you might meet the writer Mr. Derek Tangye taking a stroll along this path to Lamorna with his donkey, who appears to enjoy the walk as much as he obviously does. He and his beloved late wife Jeannie have written many books about their animals and our local life. I imagine he'd rightly call it his area too now and a favourite spot might be BOSCAWEN POINT.

BOSCAWEN POINT
– is shown on page 8 as a watercolour

non cliff top walkers return back up the Lamorna valley to the B3315; turn left

One can see both the amateur and the professional diver enjoying many an energetic hour, taking advantage of the warmth and clarity of our waters. It was one such diver who found the anchor of the ill-fated Solomon Browne lifeboat.

Tater-du stands as a land based unmanned lighthouse, built after the tragedy of three lost sailors from France. Do have a care if the weather closes in – both on land or out to sea. The (very) loudspeakers "***PEEP***" without warning! They are switched on remotely – over at the Falmouth coastguard.

PENDEEN WATCH
a lighthouse near St. Just

With a southerly wind the sound of the high pitched Tater-du can be heard all over our three parishes! A northerly will bring in the deep and slow moaning sound of the PENDEEN WATCH.

When you awake surrounded by mist, do not stop in and moan in unison with the fog horn, get dressed and feel the gentle dampness to your face. I assure you it feels pleasantly like heavy dew must feel to the plant life. Be it known that the weather on either coast can be entirely different! Often our visitors waste a whole day of their precious time not knowing that just around the corner the golden sun awaits them.

This *south* coast is favoured with early flowers and potatoes – usually by just a few precious weeks. The tiniest of meadows we see before us, even down right at the very edge of these undulating cliffs, are largely worked manually.

The meadows were extensively worked up to around the second World War, but it became more economic for the country to import rather than grow our own. During the war years the Government stretched our farmers to their full potential, while at the same time running a cheap food policy to subsidise the consumer. After the war these subsidies were reduced to the point where it became uneconomic for those farmers to continue. Some things such as, pigs and the sheer variety of orchard produce, continue to decline. Others like dairy and grain have intensified even further.

Nowadays the (European) Common Market policies require the farmer to only produce his *quota*. Milk, beef, corn and lamb are included. All this after the Government had pumped in £'s and £'s of grants to entice each farmer to overly invest, perhaps beyond his own financial means. The quota system is specified with production and markets in mind – not to the financial return that might be necessary for the farmer to be able to repay his debt. He is just not *permitted* to overproduce. I've seen milk literally taken from the cows and poured straight down the drain – such lunacy! In fact the country underproduces milk which then has to be imported…

So these rough little meadows, long given up as uneconomic, are now quietly worked as allotments. One easily regrets the progress [sic]. Think of the times people must have had working in such surroundings. Lunch in the corner. Bound to have been with a pasty and HEVVA cake, all in a basket lined with the whitest of linen. Perhaps the baby laid in a Moses basket to the foot of the hedge – for there was no excuse to stay in the house in days past. Just because the mother had a scattering of children, or flagstone floors to be scrubbed, when the man said *he* was ready for work in the meadow –

HEVVA – *sounds like heavy; it is made of flour, lard, dried fruit – some like it thin & firm, others like it slightly thicker & more fluffy*

TOUSER – *a*
hessian apron used
for dirty work

shovel over his shoulder:
> "are 'ee ready yet? 'ave on that there TOUSER
>   and 'urry up… time's going on."

In modern practice we lose the historical knowledge of the
soil and crops. Each individual field varies – only the old
farmers would know which field managed best with what crop
or use. A simple mistake of ploughing a little too deeply, in
what appears to be two identical neighbouring fields, can take
years to rectify down here in Cornwall.

This part of the coast is not walked so intensively as the access
is a little awkward with some undulating, rough and not very
visible pathways. The butterflies, birds and bees are most
numerous. I would have expected to see some lizards basking
in these warm sheltered parts but I've not. I have a family of
these at the end of Alsia lane. If you should see them, make
sure your shadow does not cover them as you approach or
these little reptiles will disappear at an unimaginable speed.

Keep an ever watchful eye for porpoise or dolphins playing
about, rolling smoothly, twisting, turning and hardly
disturbing the surface of the water. One way and then the
other. Their honk-honking calls. These lovely creatures make
me feel as like a *Peeping Tom*, as if eavesdropping on a human
family. You may see a fisherman talking to one that might
have adopted him and his boat! Although, in truth, these
beautiful creatures cause themselves and the fishing industry
great anguish when they get caught up in the great nets.

For city dwellers any of these country walks must be so
refreshing. Breeze on your face. Wind howling into
your jacket. Sea curling and swirling. Tide
thundering onto the rocks, changing that temper to
a gentle lap. In and out of the granite boulders. A
glittering ripple over the sand, lit by sun or moon.
Shag and cormorant hunched on solitary stranded
rocks. Oystercatchers sand-dancing. Gannets diving.
All this… memories to treasure for ever.

Memories of Boskenna

The fine granite entrance shows the way down to a grand private house in a leisurely setting. Though the estate has been divided and sold a number of ways, it has managed to keep a certain grandeur of its bygone days.

continue ¹/₂ mile past the Boskenna Cross; look to left for that fine granite entrance

For a very long time *Boskenna* was the family home and the estate business centre of the Paynters. I have read that the Paynter family of Burian [St. Buryan] is said to have been originally called De Camborne and to have settled at Deverell and Gwinear prior to Boskenna.

Colonel Paynter's only child Betty was a most colourful character. She loved parties and the *high life* and known to have the romantic attentions of the famous MARCONI, some 51 years her senior, when she was only 14. Through this friendship she became the first woman to make a wireless broadcast from the Lizard Point across the wide expanse of water over to America.

MARCONI – credited with developing early wireless telegraphy

My memories here as a child are of a grassy bank overlooking the lawn. There was a fete, in aid of the war effort I think. All ladies and a sprinkling of children. A lovely sunny day. Suddenly a lady with a loud cheerful voice appeared in a pale blue chiffon dress. From the gentle way it flowed in the warm breeze it might have been pure silk. All business of the day stopped to gaze upon something we'd never seen before, Miss Betty *wearing* a large 'branch' of bananas – shoulder slung! I do not recall who won this raffle prize, but I do remember her talking for a long time about her trip overseas to actually fetch this bunch of bananas. We listened with intent rapture to her every word. Of the climate, the vegetation & the foreign way of life. Don't forget that even just fifty years ago it would have been very unusual to have needed to travel beyond Penzance.

The White Pony of Trevedran

*Trevedran Farm is
seen just ahead and
to the left through the
trees when you get to
the bottom of the
next valley*

The night the land of Lyonesse disappeared it is said a
Vyvyan (Vivian) ancestor called Trevelyan (Trevillian) rode
a white pony through the night to reach safety from the
rising sea. Realising his homeland was now to be no more
than the ocean bottom for ever, he decided to settle here at
Trevedran (Trevidran or Treviddren).

TRELOWARREN –
near Helston

From then on he always kept a white pony bridled and
saddled in the stable. The family name was carried through
to the TRELOWARREN house by John [son of Ralph Vyvyan]
marrying Honor Ferrers in 1426. Descendants kept up this
tradition until quite recent times.

*Trevedran Farm
with its thatched roof*

I'm told that the family motto *"Dum Vivimus Vivamus"*
translates as *"While we live, let us live"*. They certainly did that

in the past. In 1328 Richard and his sons, William and Hugh, were three of the forty one people excommunicated in an *incident* with the Rev. Richard Beaurre of St. Just. One son [William] was absolved by the Bishop some eight years later.

The Trevedran thatched house still stands; carefully being looked after by the Nicholls family, whose family have farmed here for almost sixty years. Their view is of across the narrow wooded valley known as St. Loy, which is very popular with walkers when the profuse wild daffodils and bluebells start flowering.

One would imagine it always to have been so.

Queensway

This story is told in all sincerity, but to which Queen it refers I am not at all sure.

It starts with a great excitement in the village of St. Buryan. For sometime it had been rumoured the Queen was to pass through the village and today was to be the day. Everyone was dressed in their *Sunday Best*. So too the families of outlying

the pretty wooded valley of St. Loy can be followed to the sea; it is not well signed; tends to get quite muddy; ending with a somewhat slippery & testing climb to get down to the sea; the cove consists entirely of rocks and boulders

farms… well, all those who could be spared at least!
Excited gatherings in the square. Church bells pealing.
In the Middle Ages to have ever even hoped to see the Queen
must have been rare. For her to arrive in one's village must
have been unique! This Queen is thought to have come ashore
at Mousehole and was to visit the Logan Rock and Land's End.

(I expect we were just as excited at our own Queen Elizabeth's
Silver Jubilee service; the church was filled to overflowing.
Long unseen neighbours talked to; friendships renewed.)

BURNEWHALL —
sounds like bruh-nowl,
also spelt as Burnuhal
or Barnhual; its gate
is to the left at the
bottom of a short hill

The Queen's entourage must have kept to the coastal road, via
Lamorna past Boskenna Cross. At BURNEWHALL GATE there is
a little stream. An old Granny was busy gutting fish. Our fine
lady spoke from her horse:
"May I come in and rest awhile at your home."
Whereupon the old Granny said:
"Well 'ere take the key out of my pocket. My hands are dirty, you
go up an' I'll come up – join you in a minute."

The old Granny picked up her fish, rinsed off her knife &
hands and followed her unexpected visitors home. She saw
to it that her Ladyship had her best cushions, then served
her and the others in the group with fish, cakes, honey and
Cornish cream. Her visitors had a great time. As the Queen
left she gave the old Granny some keepsakes in gratitude.

QUEENSWAY —
may be walked from
Burnewhall Farm
down to the cliffs; it
joins the coastal path
a little way out of
Penberth Cove

The Queen's entourage continued, past the present
farmhouse, down across the cliff and on into Penberth.
The path is even today called QUEENSWAY.

When squire Pender returned from the village, the old Granny
told him about the visit. He could hardly believe it until she
showed him the ornaments that had been given to her.

So the people in the village did not see the Queen!
It has been suggested that the Queen was actually
Catherine Braganza of Portugal, betrothed to Charles II, on
her way to their marriage around 1662.

Legend also has it that the son of Charles I, that is Charles [Prince of Wales] and later Charles II, hid at Burnewhall, Nanquidno and Kelynack before fleeing to France from Sennen Cove. It is also said that the old Granny was the grandmother Pender of the William Noy [Noye] who died 1634 and was Attorney General to King Charles I. As the story relates to one spoken of by grandparents of Noy, I feel that the Queen must have been one from much earlier.

turn left at junction B3283 – B3315; head for St. Levan on the B3315

(please note that Boscean Farm lane is for walkers only)

St. Levan

Magical Penberth

Here is a rambling lane down which one may walk or drive. Its very narrowness exudes a flavour of mystery and magic.

'ignore' the left turn signed Penberth(!); carry on a few yards to do a 'U' turn at the wide entry to the turn for Treen; then turn into that narrow Penberth lane

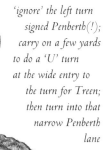

Now, here and there, one can steal glimpses of a beautiful homestead. Springtime the primroses peep from many a little crevice in the hedges. It's to the late Commander Favell's mother we have to thank for this, as she used her staff to plant out the valley's lane.

Some way down we pass the unusual gatehouse. Every time I pass it I recall how my inquisitive nature has a habit of leading me into other people's business! Visitors, who were staying at my farmhouse, asked:

"Why are there flags draped along the hedges by the gatehouse?".
I replied:
"No idea. Possibly the Favells have some important people calling".
Next day the lunchtime news announced Prince Charles had made a private visit to our Minack Theatre. Inquisitively I telephoned the late Mrs. Favell to ask whether the flags were up to greet the Prince. She gave a hearty laugh and said:
"We always put the flags up when one of our three daughters is expected home."
So if you've seen the flags flying, you'll now know the reason.

car users should arrange themselves appropriately at the 'end' of the lane — the final section does not permit public traffic, walkers are welcome

Penberth has been home to four generations of the Favell family — one well known and dearly liked in the area. These lovely gardens are occasionally opened to the public on behalf of charities. It was in the gardens I remember winning a large iced cake in a fete raffle.

This was a much sought after prize soon after the war — anything with icing was indeed rare. To save a bit of valuable petrol ration Mrs. Greet [Alsia cottage], mother, sisters & I walked a part of the way home. I was unwisely entrusted with the holding of this cake while we rested at the steep hairpin bend climbing out the valley. Mother then took charge of the cake — less a few knobs of the icing! She never scolded me or even mentioned the missing icing. I bet she had quite a chuckle to herself watching my guilty reactions. Since rearing my own family I've been in similar situations.

Down at the cove

Father, as a boy at the Trendrennen Farm, had made many friends. On some summer evenings he would drive us all down to Penberth cove to see the fishermen in and meet up with his friends. My sisters and I would play among the boulders – poking at the innocent little sea creatures, finding shells and looking for seaweeds of many different textures and colours. None of which ever looked half as nice once out of the water!

Trendrennen Farm is nearby – over the hill near Porthcurno

At this busy little fishing cove, I've counted as many as 23 boats hauled up upon the slipway, as much as it can hold.

The morning sun glows into the cove, but my favourite time is in the late evening. The busy putter of little boats. The ringing chatter of fishermen. The screeching call of gulls. The rhythmic lapping of waves. In such an intimate cove the world seems so at ease. Dusk settles.

The old winch man would be leaning on the hand-capstan, idly looking on, as the modern two stroke engine took the strain positioning the boats ready for launching.
The positions would depend on which were to be next to go fishing. You might just imagine how this cove and the many crevices around served to fuel the old smugglers' tales. This is the very spot to sit awhile and listen to this story of old.

it is here in the cove at Penberth that we might rejoin our more energetic fellow explorers as they finish their coastal path walk from Lamorna!

The story of Boscean Farm & Boy Frank

BOSCEAN FARM –
as seen from the
start of the lane

Now Boy Frank [Lanyon] lived at BOSCEAN FARM, which is the farm on top of the hill behind you. There is a breathtaking view overlooking the valley of Penberth and the ever changing temperament of the sea. This forms the background of Gran's story. I always used to think that she knew the people personally, only later finding out of the story's true age [ℂ].

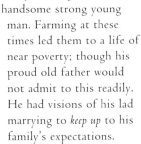

The Lanyon family were an elderly couple. Their only child Boy Frank grew to be a handsome strong young man. Farming at these times led them to a life of near poverty; though his proud old father would not admit to this readily. He had visions of his lad marrying to *keep up* to his family's expectations.

His mother was getting older and needed help with the chores. So it was arranged for her cousin's daughter Nancy should work for them. Her father, Mr. Trenoweth, was the miller at Alsia which was just up the valley. Its small but profitable farm had a pleasant orchard. There were the smells of the blossom in spring and of its fruits in autumn. These encouraged many people to pass through the valley.

So Nancy left this sheltered vale for the windswept farm of Boscean. The elder Lanyons saw little of the rest of the world and Boy Frank & Nancy seldom went further from home than to join in the community games. Up at St. Buryan these games of strength and agility, e.g. tug-of-war, Cornish wrestling and the like, were as much admired by the high born young ladies of the area as by the others . They'd witness these sports without shame because they took place in daylight!

(would this be an early form of the 'Chippendales'?)

The attentions of these eligible ladies for a good looking young man such as Boy Frank of Boscean were in vain. Being so light-hearted and fancy-free he'd now lost his heart to the young, beautiful and sweet tempered Nancy.

As time went by he scarcely left the farm but to escort her to see her parents at Alsia Mill – a place always full of laughter and gaiety where people of all classes mingled while waiting for their grain to be milled. There they'd tell stories, exchange news, sing ballads and often have an impromptu dance on the floor of the mill to the music from the miller's daughters.

Little did either family think of the friendship as anything other than platonic. Indeed the true feelings were not brought to light until old man Hugh Lanyon of Boscean decided it was time to have a *heart to heart* talk with his son. He and his mother were getting on in years, so perhaps it would be time for him to consider mixing more with the gentry of the area – with a view to finding a suitable bride. After all, he was a man of good looks with a strong physique and would bring the attention of many a fair maiden.

To the father's complete astonishment his son simply left him aghast on declaring he would marry Nancy for love rather than into the Noy's, Pender's or Tresilians for money.

Old man Lanyon flew into a rage, saying that he would rather follow his son to the grave than see him marry *down* to one such as Nancy Trenoweth. Such was his stubborn pride, like many a family of these times. He had forgotten Nancy was his cousin's daughter [on his wife's side] and her miller father was of a far better pocket than himself.

Nancy was sent home. Though it was no hardship to have her back, the miller's pride had been hurt and a family feud ensued. When Boy Frank called to see Nancy that night, he was ordered away. He returned to Boscean saddened.

The young lovers secretly schemed, meeting often — sometimes in the orchard, sometimes at the Holy Well. Both mothers often collaborated with these clandestine meetings.

there is a picture of the Alsia Holy Well on page 26

As she dare not tell her sisters and other girls of the hamlet, they mistook her apparent reserve as *Pride* and they got up to tricks. They took malicious fun in watching for Boy Frank's arrival, be it from Alsia corner through the valley lane from Bosanketh, or from across the Crean moorland. Then they would make it their business to tell father, who would then make it his affair to see him off his land.

Family life at Boscean became unbearable, he continued to work hard, but all his meals were in silence. Such a difference, for when Nancy was on the farm he'd hardly leave. Now he couldn't wait to get away. There were stories that he'd spend long hours riding his favourite colt, also at the inn of St. Buryan.

Boy Frank decided to go to sea and do a bit of *free trading* — not an uncommon thing to do. He was a natural leader, quickly putting together a crew.

Nancy met him early one autumn morning – once more at Alsia bottoms near the Holy Well. She accompanied him down to Penberth Cove where his comrades & craft awaited. Gleaming in the sunlight it glided silently out of the cove. It would be the last time for many of the crew.

Months passed without news. Anxious enquiries were made to various ports. From Falmouth they heard of a rumour that just such a craft as Boy Frank's had been confronted by a pirate ship – a scourge of the Mediterranean. People from Spain and Portugal had spoken of a broken vessel and of a crew in great distress being driven out to sea with no provisions.

On learning of the grave import of the rumour, old man Lanyon's stubborn anger turned to grief at the thought of the loss of his only son. To allay his grief he thought to replace this void with what his family had earlier treated as their daughter. To this extent, he humbled himself so low as to beg the miller Trenoweth to allow Nancy to return. Wretched indeed was the visible plight of the Lanyons but the miller could not bring himself to allow her to return to Boscean.

Sadly, it was now obvious that Nancy was expecting a child.

Nancy's child

Nancy's grandmother took her under her wing. She was known as the Wise Woman of Alsia (nee Johanna Pender) and skilled in the making of potions and ointments, preparing them from herbs and flowers collected off the moors. She also grew much in her cottage garden which would encourage bees. Honey was of great importance in those days, both to sweeten food and in the making of medicines and creams. My Gran gave me to understand that this small cottage was in the yard above the mill. It was very small and the garden highly perfumed, but now it is gone. Here Nancy's baby – a boy – was born.

It was to this cottage that Boy Frank's parents fruitlessly came to Nancy in order to ask her to return and to bring their lost son's unknown child.

So as not to be a burden to her grandmother, she obtained work as a girl IN SERVICE with a kindly couple in Kemyel. The Trenoweth's now gladly took care of their grandchild. She often walked back after a full day's work just to see her son.

A sealed bottle floated into *Pedn-vounder*. Inside, a message told of events some months previous and asked to be passed to a Nancy Trenoweth of Alsia. There was the name of a dreaded pirate ship and those of Boy Frank and his comrades. It all served to confirm Nancy's dread and that of the rumour.

She tried to relieve her sorrow with all manner of potions and spells. Every night she would go up the barn steps at Kemyel and look out to the sea. She could scarcely believe her Boy Frank was dead. That night, so very calm after a monstrous storm the night before, there was a sound of a horse's hooves getting ever closer...

Suddenly in the moonlight she could make out the outline of her Boy Frank. Approaching quickly he swept her up with a strong arm onto the horse with him. Like the wind they flew. Over a stream. Up Trevider way. Tearing into St. Buryan.

By now she realised it was not her Boy Frank, but his ghost, and she shrieked in terror to the blacksmith to pull her free. As he did so her dress was torn. The ghostly horse and its rider raced over the church graveyard wall and disappeared into the night. Be it known that the villagers kept this event away from the Boscean Lanyons.

After being out in the previous night's fierce storm and, along with the shock of being caught up with this apparition, all these events led her to suffer a dreadful pneumonia.

That storm also saw a vessel in dire distress.

At Porthguarnon Cove, near Porthcurno, sailors' voices were heard amid the crashing of waves and the gale's roaring.

People raced along the cliff to see how they might assist. They saw a crew struggling in the surf, desperately trying to reach safety upon the rocky ledges. Hastily they dropped ropes down the cliff side.

It was Boy Frank and his crew who were in such peril. They were returning home after two years and had been loaded with riches somehow gained from a pirate ship. Their brave captain Boy Frank was the last up, his strength almost gone. Rescuers helped him and, on hearing his mother's voice, he weakly asked that they might take him home. So very bruised and scarred was he that his parents could barely recognise him. The agitation was so great that they took little note of his request to fetch Nancy. He died without her. In fact they thought no more of it until after he was laid to rest in the St. Buryan Church graveyard.

Going home, when they got to the Goonmenheere stile, old man Lanyon and his wife were overcome with an obligation to go above the family feud. They turned to go to Alsia to see their grandson and to tell the miller's family that, in their grief, they had neglected to fulfil Boy Frank's last request to send for his Nancy.

On their way they called in at the grandmother's little cottage. She got the robust youngster and placed him onto old man Lanyon's lap. Now the tears of sorrow really fell – for her sad news was that Nancy also lay dead.

Both families agreed that she should be buried in the same grave as the love of her life. As fate would have it, Boy Frank's favourite colt was found dead in Boscean farmyard the day after the appearance of the graveyard apparition.

(return back up the lane to the B3315; left and left again almost immediately up to Treen)

Note that Gran (as are all the old storytellers) was adamant in that the scrap of dress, that the blacksmith had seen torn off when he had hauled Nancy from the spirit horse, was mysteriously found *inside* the grave when it was reopened for Nancy to be interred with Boy Frank...

Now we'll leave the quiet of the valley of Penberth and continue around and up into the hamlet of Treen.

The Logan Rock

LOGAN ROCK – *means 'rocking stone'*

exploring the hamlet should reveal the way to the Logan(!)

Treen has a nice Public House serving all sorts of fare. While enjoying your refreshments you can review the history of the LOGAN ROCK, as there are many pictures & writings displayed. A chat with the locals might reveal the saucier of the tales!

Past the village store and Post Office there is a car park from which you can start your walk, over several fields, through to the cliffs and on towards the Logan Rock.

It was in the ℂ that we are given to understand it was an *effortless task* to set the stone rocking. Around that time I believe our William Borlase is reported to have said:

"It is impossible that any lever, or indeed force applied in a mechanical manner, can remove the rocking stone from its position"

the path is across several fields; there are NT signs nearer to the spot; the actual Rock takes a bit of 'getting up to'

A certain Lieutenant Oliver Goldsmith of the Royal Navy was in the locality and he just *had* to prove him wrong. With his seafaring training he indeed managed to topple the rock. The resultant consternation incurred the wrath of the Admiralty and he was *ordered* to restore the situation.

a visitor most ably confirming that our Logan Rock actually does still rock

The Logan Rock weighs in the region of 84 tons and now lay at the bottom of its pinnacle! It was no mean feat and weighed equally heavily on his career and his purse.

So the rock still *Logans*, albeit less easily. It needs a sturdy body and steady mind to actually climb up to it, but it is possible and it does rock.

The immediate area was known in olden times as *Treryn Dinas* and said to have been an Iron Age fortress.

Iron Age 450BC – 43AD

We continue around to Porthcurno – through the top end of St. Levan. This oddity occurs as most of *St. Levan* is up here but the actual St. Levan Church is way down the Porthcurno valley, up around past the Minack & further around the cliff.

Porthcurno

Go down into the valley of Porthcurno. At one time almost the whole valley was owned and run by Cable & Wireless, who

earlier used it as a wireless & cable landing site and later as an intensive full time training centre. A telecommunications museum is being planned so do ask around.

At the bottom there is a large municipal car park for the popular beach at Porthcurno.

After that there is a very narrow lane with a steep climb to get to the Minack and on through to the actual St. Levan Church. The privately run *Mariners' Lodge* hotel (on the hairpin bend) commands absolutely terrific views – teas may be available.

The Minack Theatre

It was Miss Rowena Cade who, in 1928, tempted the elements with an outstanding performance of Shakespeare's *A Midsummer Night's Dream* down in the nearby valley of Crean. I've been told by *actual* performers and members of the audience that it was truly memorable! From this the idea of the Minack was born. Miss Cade and her gardener set about carving the theatre straight out of this cliff. There is a Rowena Cade exhibition centre which details the beginnings of the theatre and portrays the achievements of this remarkable lady. It is well worth the visit.

People are drawn from all over the world to these open air performances – with the sea for a backcloth & the raw elements for its atmosphere. Utterly sensational magic!

Armed with hampers, flasks of soup, tea and sometimes whisky, blankets and cushions; chattering excitedly they would wend their way down the cliff steps to join friends and parties already seated. This is a spot of sheer enchantment. The sea provides a continually moving backdrop and the gathering dusk an atmosphere. Basking sharks cruise lazily. Seals and dolphins provide occasional surprises. Returning fishing trawlers are always seen burbling home. At times even the moonlight complements the spectacle.

...Comedy of Errors
I believe (1992)

Your visit to the area is really not complete without taking in a performance at the Minack Theatre.

Views from the Minack

*the Logan Rock can
be seen here on top
(to the centre)*

Looking nearer is the area known as Pedn-vounder – now an *accepted* naturist area. Not so in the 1930's, when an infamous man came to live in this area and who decided nude bathing was for him. The local men found it so distasteful that he should be so offensive to their wives and children that they stoned him off the beach on a number of occasions. Oh my, how things have changed!

If you are on the lovely cliff bottom sand do keep a wary eye on an incoming tide. The sand banks vary considerably and you can become quickly isolated. Even locals have been trapped. A cousin of mine was caught with her sister-in-law and her two children and decided to wait out the tide. The tide would not be high but it was lapping at their feet and the two young children were frightened. Their menfolk became alarmed by nightfall and arrived with friends from Treen and Penberth. It was indeed a relieving sight to see what looked like a chinese lantern procession bobbing up and down as the rescue party walked towards them.

Nearer still is Porthcurno beach whose sand is of a coarser nature, being made entirely of tiny crushed shell pieces. At high tide there is a pronounced incline which can make it very dangerous to an unsuspecting paddler. Strong swimmers only! Visitors were once amazed to see people running around with palm trees and later discovered, not that the Cornish were mad, but just another film crew among the sand dunes.

the view from around the Logan Rock and across Pedn-vounder to Porthcurno Beach; the Minack Theatre nestles halfway up the cliff side opposite

As a child I remember being told not to tell any strangers where we saw secret communications cables being laid under the beach. I believe these went to far off places such as the USA, Australia and India. I can only think that a shadowy fear of sabotage left over from wartime years could be the reason.

Looking up the valley, past the Cable & Wireless station and its aerial farm, you will see the crofting land of Trendrennen Farm. On the field known as *Downs Bertha* is an ancient burial area, but I can't find anything further. Though the family has been resident for several generations, few details were passed down.

My ancestors here at Trendrennen (Trengothal too) were always ready for business when the opportunity might arrive! Grandmother Hocking baked the station's bread, buns and cakes. Chuckling, aunt May told me a story of one January's particularly heavy snow fall. The boys could not use the road to deliver the baking. Being adventurous and, so as not to lose trade, they scrubbed the farm wheelbarrow, laid a white board on top and wrapped the baking in linen. Grandmother's orders were that the boys push the barrow across the fields and the girls dress up for delivery.

aunt May here as a young girl aged 15½ years

You may recall reading further back of the St. Buryan Races at Down's Barn, of how the family was asked not to continue them there after one of the Care family had died. These races continued on other farms – Trendrennen being one. Aunt May told me of how she and the family spent hours clearing the course of stones and other debris that might endanger the racers. Grandfather Hocking entered their old farm horse *Old Polly* in one of the lower classes. The whole family madly cheered her on. She did her best but wasn't terribly successful - despite running on her home ground.

There is a narrow and awkward path down to Porthchapel – a beach which has become very popular of late. Its access is not that suitable for the very young or elderly. Wonder if that's why it's popular, are they trying to tell me something?

left out of Minack's access lane; continue along the lane; Porthchapel is to the left

St Levan Church

St. Selevan is thought to be a Celtic Saint – even a brother to St. Just, through whom his name can also be connected with a number of places in Brittany. On landing at the cove of Porthchapel he is understood to have conducted baptisms from a holy well nearby – there are also ruins of a chapel. The present granite church used to be called St. Selevan and dates from ℭ – ℭ. It was built sympathetically into the natural incline of the land and is a well-loved church whose fabric has been kept in good repair. Inside there are carved bench ends – some new, some old. More recent ones, in memory of local people, depict something of their lives. There is a simple Norman font and a pulpit [1752]. A solid slate floor (possibly Delabole) appears to exaggerate the darkness, contrasting with the clarity of the stained glass windows.

there are discrete signs to aid car parking & others that point out the way to the beach

Outside, a large stone appears to be split. In pre-Christianity it was known as a Holy Rock. The story is that St. Selevan used to sit on it after tiring of fishing. One day he gave it a blow with his staff and the rock cracked right through!
He made a prophesy in prayer that:

When with panniers astride
A pack horse can ride
Through St. Selevan's Stone
The world will be done.

Judging by the space between the parts of the stone we will be safe from Armageddon for some time yet.

There are some interesting and unusually designed headstones in the graveyard. Some belong to those who perished in the wrecks of the *Aurora* and of the *Khyber*.

(Richard Wetheral)

The brig' *Aurora* floundered off Land's End in 1811. Legend has it that, from the Isles of Scilly Captain's grave, there is the ghostly sound of the *Aurora's* bell. Those who hear it are doomed to die within the year. So perhaps pass this one by quickly!

The *Khyber* of Liverpool was shattered, going down very quickly in 1905. A communal grave holds the 23 who perished. Dr. Jago (a grandfather to our own St. Just practice's Dr. Jago) was called to that scene, where he helped the 3 survivors. After the shipwreck a broken plate was found on the beach. The picture of a young girl on it was so pretty that the finder had it repaired and it was hung up at his cottage in Porthgwarra. Years later a lady visited and she turned out to be that very girl. She said that the plate was to have been a present from her sweetheart. Sadly that sailor was one who was lost that night.

the route for the coastal path around to Porthgwarra is reasonably clear but some might consider sections of it just slightly tricky

We can now either walk a slightly precarious coastal path, or drive around and down to the sea at Porthgwarra.

Porthgwarra harbour

I call Porthgwarra a *morning* beach. When the tide is out, you have a little plot of soft sand along with the boulders. A parents' dream as small children can safely play, so too the picturesque cottages are a painter's dream. When the morning sun reflects off the sea, it is like the glitter of a million diamonds. The shallow waves ripple in amongst the boulders and onto the tiny plot of sand. The harbour entrance is much like Penberth but smaller, with fewer boats and a steeper slipway. The sandy beach may also be approached by an *exciting* tunnel through the solid granite cliff side.

In 1978 an inhabitant of a harbour side cottage awoke in the early dawn sunshine and noted a large yacht far off. Drifting back to sleep he was suddenly reawakened with a crashing sound coming from the harbour. He recalled his

driving around requires you to retrace your way back up to the main B3315 & then to turn left towards Lands' End; at the Polgigga junction turn left at the sign to Porthgwarra

(this journey can be slow if there is much traffic — there are few passing places!)

absolute amazement of the sight of that yacht — as if almost in his room. The wreck of beautiful *Esperanca* practically filled the view from his window. Mr. Preben Peterson, his wife and little child, had fallen asleep after long tiring watches through a spell of bad weather during the long voyage from Santos, Brazil. The 30 ton ferro-concrete hulled yacht was lodged firmly on the rocks and proved very difficult to raise. He ran into financial problems with the subsequent expenses. They had been on their way back home to Denmark. Locals raised funds in the region of £2,500, donated all manner of articles to restock family & their boat and tradesmen assisted with appropriate services.

Certainly a very different tale from those told of our smuggling and wrecking history!

The story of a little lad

*7 cottages were built by the Jacksons in the 1880's, one cost **less** than £100!*

It was on a normal busy washday [Monday of course] at the cottage nearest the cove's edge. Mrs. Jackson had rinsed out the washtub, hurriedly left it *open end up* on the rocks to bleach out and then continued with the remaining chores.

Later Mr. Jackson returned with his two brothers from sea commenting:
  "Something afloat out Runnel's way.
  Didn't see Ernest, where's he playing to now?"
Back came the reply:
  "Playing by the rocks,
  near the washtub."

the Runnelstone is a marker buoy

Puzzled, father and brothers nipped outside, for they hadn't seen the familiar Monday washday tub outside — nor their little four year old lad. Alarmed they ran around the cottage calling out loudly. But there was no tub... no Ernest either.

Looking carefully they could still see that floating *something* out towards Runnelstone — some two miles offshore.

Father said:
  "Mother, get some help and search the shoreline.
   We'll go out and check that thing out there."
They fetched the boat out and rowed as fast as the oars would
allow. As they got nearer, that something became Mother's
washtub bobbing gently. Once alongside, *what a relief*, there was
little Ernest fast asleep and certainly quite unaware of the
distress he had inadvertently caused!

Our 'boy' Ernest was the father to the Mrs. Lilly Chapple who
once owned the Jacksons's large grocery shop in St. Buryan.

*Jacksons' Store is
still trading*

From the Porthgwarra car park one takes a gently climbing
walk past the big and very sturdily built coastguard cottages.
The recently closed *Gwennap Head* Coastguard lookout post is
found at the top. Hereabouts the currents from the
English Channel meet those sweeping around Cornwall from
the Atlantic Ocean. The turbulence can be quite dramatic.
There are many Newlyn fishermen who can tell you true
stories of almost incredible freak waves that can form here.
Some of the classes of trawler have open sterns that are quite
vulnerable at particular times. When one of these monstrous
freak waves suddenly arrives, to dump tons of seawater straight
down into the open holds, the effect tends to be catastrophic.

*follow the narrow
lane that goes gently
uphill from the back
of the car park*

The walkways are fairly easy, especially if you keep to the
high side. Give yourself plenty of time, as you will be waylaid
with the command-
ing views, the
families of porp-
oises at play and
the variation of
flowers at your feet.

*Gwennap Head after
a flurry of rain*

The cliff walk takes
you past Nanjizal
and goes on around
to Land's End.

Nanjizal

*some parts of the
walk hereabouts can
be a little awkward*

The surface of the beach here varies greatly from year to year. One year a great mass of rocky boulders, the next all these are covered with carpets of fine grained sand – not a rock in sight!

On asking Gran why, she replied:

"Once upon a time a man had done something very wrong. His punishment was to carry sand from here to Porthcurno and back again – until the end of time."

It was on this beach that our *Buryan Bell* was found.

Now if you are feeling energetic you might continue along the path towards Land's End. The purple hues of the heather cover cliff and moorland. It is a paradise for the bees and also the insect hunting little birds. All forever searching for food. Flitting around – even quite close to our feet. Here too there are gannets. They dive 200ft. into the sea and barely disturb the surface. Gulls in numbers too numerous to mention. You might see the great surface shadow of a cruising basking shark, which can be some 40ft. long! This is no *Jaws* as the species is only interested in food of the plankton and shrimp variety.

Ahead of you are the lands of those *Vingoes of Trevilley.*

Land's End

Further still, one can see the outline of the Land's End Hotel
and its modern exhibition complex. Land's End can feasibly

take the whole day for a family to enjoy. It boasts a variety of
attractions and facilities, many of which are designed to be
enjoyed in all weathers.

If you can, do take care to keep to existing paths while
exploring around Land's End and its immediate coastline.
The location is so popular that significant erosion has
occurred, from which it is all too slow to recover.

It is the *Longships* lighthouse that can be seen
just over a mile out to sea. If you know your
way around maps you can also see the *Wolf Rock*
lighthouse and the *Seven Stones* lightship.

After retracing our steps back to Porthgwarra,
let us now go to Bottoms.

Bottoms

return to the B3315 at Polgigga; turn right; shortly take the next left at the fork (signed to Bottoms & Crean)

There is a short riverside walk from Bottoms down to Penberth valley. Recently a vineyard has been started. Because of the sheltered nature of the valley, the trees here are of the highest in the three parishes. With a sparse human population the area sustains a good range of wildlife – badger, rabbit, fox and the occasional stoat. Also many little birds, wren, robin, wagtails (pied, yellow & grey), might fly past as you wander through this glorious vale. A tapping noise that you may hear might be one such bird knocking a snail from its shell; or a woodpecker fooling you with his laugh-like call. At eventide you'll hear the noisy return of the crows and rooks. Bats flying so low that you'll think they'll hit you, but you'll be safe enough.

the school is to the left - a little way up from the bottom of the steep hill

Bottoms is a sleepy hamlet. It has a school with a bell that hangs high but is not in general use. The beautiful building is of dressed granite set in a school yard surrounded by trees. It is the property of the Methodists and has been threatened with closure for the past forty years but every time being reprieved. This was possibly due to its use by the families of the Cable & Wireless employees at Porthcurno. That place has now been closed down, so uncertainly is back in the air.

The milk factory at Bottoms

at the bottom, the large house to your half-left

This large stout building has now been beautifully converted into a private dwelling. The area in front of it used to look somewhat naked, many of its trees succumbed to the dreaded Dutch elm beetle disease, but nature has recovered beautifully.

As children, my cousin Heather and I, spent literally hours picking blackberries in its grounds. Running in and out of, what was then, derelict buildings. Shrieking and calling, just to hear the echo resounding within. I thought of doing just that when I had reason to call sometime ago. I did hesitate... the reason was not just that my age was against me but also of the concern of Sir Darrel-Bates and his wife who lived there!

My father recalled his own father driving the horse and cart loaded with Trendrennen milk to the factory. Along the way the children would be dropped off at the school. Talking of dropping off, there was also an incident on the winding little Gilley Lane. Alsia's farm worker, Mr. Clemmens, spilt all the milk over that lane when a wheel fell off the cart. That was a serious affair in those days. Milk produced at Trengothal in Gran's day used to go there, as did that of Alsia in my own father's day. Nowadays the St. Erth factory processes milk.

(...Old Polly again)

Gilley Lane is a very narrow lane from Bosfranken Farm down into Bottoms

Imagine. It must have been quite a busy area in the mornings with horses, carts and later the few early tractors. What a contrast to the now sleepy atmosphere.

Gran perfected her dairy skills [butter and cheese making] to meet the rising demand of the markets that were, by this time, starting to adopt uniform sizes and packaging. So too hygiene was being taken more into account. This old photograph shows Gran, seated on the grass to the centre front, with her classmates from the old milk factory.

Trengothal – Gran's birthplace

Past the old milk factory and part of the way up this hill there stands the 'chocolate box' thatched cottage *Whistle*.

Roger   Joyce   Gran   Mary (Mum)

GRAN – *at the St. Buryan village hall – the occasion was my sister Joyce's 21st birthday party*

The narrow lane beside it is a lonely mile long and it goes all the way to Trengothal Farm, where Gran was born.

Trengothal is a settlement of a few dwellings and extensive farm buildings. It used to be described as a *halfway staging point* – such as for an early postal service. The lane then would have gone right through to Mayon [Sennen].

Gran knew how to feed a cow, so that it would then produce milk for her to turn into butter. She also learnt how to rear a chicken from an egg, to that of the art of presenting it at the table with such elegance that the television version of *Mrs. Bucket/Bouquet* would have been delighted to see at one of her 'candlelight dinners'.

So too the sort of obedience required to serve the residential senior company staff (Cable & Wireless) who had booked up the whole of her big farmhouse. That company later built their own company houses down in the valley of Porthcurno. Gran explained that the service would have been on par with that seen on the screen versions of *Upstairs/Downstairs* and other dramas set in Victorian England.

The family still found time to socialise, though being related to a large number of local families no doubt helped. Gran initially

got engaged to a PK student. Later she realised that she would
have been expected to travel the world, following her husband's
tour of duty requirements. She was then engaged to [Tresidder]
Mr. Henry Murley. Unfortunately this was not to be, though
her peers often said they were a lovely couple. He foolishly
abstracted his own tooth with an unsterilised pig's tooth
remover! Pyaemia formed in his gums. In those days it was fatal.
Her third engagement led to her marriage to Mr. David Rogers
[formerly Trembethow, Lelant]. She raised a large family,
tended paying guests at home and worked hard on their land.
Her sons even had to order her back home from milking – when
she was in her 70's. Just as well she had good health.

*there are many
Cornish C&W
wives scattered all
around the world...
(the letters PK refer
to the telegraphic code
by which C&W
at Porthcurno was
known globally)*

The wedding of Annie Humphrys

This 1911 wedding photo is of Gran's sister, Annie, who was
married from Trengothal to the St. Levan carpenter
Mr. Henry Humphrys. She was the first bride to be taken to
St Levan Church
BY CAR!

*Gran – the left of the
three actually seated
on the grass*

passementerie —
decorated trimming
of gimp cord, beads
and braid

Her bridal gown was of brown crepe de Chine trimmed with white satin under lace and PASSEMENTERIE . These anemone-like trimmings adorned the neck and sleeve edges, with similar double panels at the front. Her crinoline hat was trimmed in white satin with chiffon and also with wings. The three sisters were all dressed in white silk; the young one in the white hat and the other two (including Gran) had dark.

The bride's *going away* outfit was a mixed tweed costume and a seal skin hat. The honeymoon was spent in Plymouth.

WEDDING
BREAKFAST —

the celebration meal
following the wedding
service — as, strictly
speaking, food is not
taken before the
Communion

I wonder if, at the WEDDING BREAKFAST, whether *Jugged Hare* was on the menu? It was so at Gran's, who like Annie, came back to this impressive farmhouse at Trengothal after her own wedding in the following year (1912).

Jugged Hare recipe:

Preparations:
Paunch & skin the hare.
Wipe with dry cloth.
Cut into neat pieces
(drain blood into basin).
Fry in dripping until light brown.

Stock:
1½lb bones, 1 carrot & 1 onion
4pt water, 2 bay leaves & 4 cloves
Pepper & salt to taste.

Forcemeat balls:
½lb steak cut into small strips
½lb ham cut into small strips
Fry together in dripping.
With 8 tablespoons of
breadcrumbs, add parsley,
½ teaspoon mixed herbs
and 1 lemon (rind and juice).
Pepper & salt to taste.
Form into 12 meatballs.

Finally:
Place the hare & forcemeat balls
into a casserole dish.
Add 4 cloves.
Pepper & salt to taste.
Add stock.
Bring to boil; simmer for 3 – 4 hrs.

Gravy:
Strain liquid produced on simmer.
Add 2oz plain flour.
Blend with blood.
Bring back to the boil.
Add ½ glass of Port.

Presentation:
Use a large platter.
Hare pieces in the centre surrounded
by the forcemeat balls, on a bed
of watercress & red jelly [jam].
Pour another ½ glass of Port over
the centre hare pieces.

With a full size hare this recipe should satisfy a large family.

Farming in bygone days

Let's try to discover the secrets we have lost.
What is the secret of such contentment in
this area? In truth it has the rugged beauty
so appealing to towns' folk. Others might
talk of bleakness beyond belief, when the
winter gales roar in, seemingly from all sides.

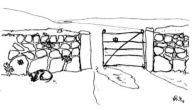

The horseman

The horseman was the most important man on a farm in those
bygone years [1900's]. After all, the horse was indeed *the* most
necessary of animals since the oxen. It would pull the farm
implements for work and also be required for pleasure, such as
to be able to go out socialising into the villages on the cart.

*…let's not forget
dear Old Polly*

He would have to rise by 4:30am in the summer and perhaps
two hours later in the winter. This would be *every* day – there
were no five day weeks in those times!

The first job would be to give the horses their fodder; then to
clean out around them, checking their feet and such, or for
any coughing. It was so important that his charges should be
in the best of health for the long day ahead. There would be
the smell of sweet hay, of BRASSO, of the oils that would keep
the leather soft and supple (so as not to rub the horse).
When all was well, it was off to the groom's own breakfast.

BRASSO – *a metal
polish still in quite
widespread use*

On returning to the stable he would brush and comb their
coats to a high sheen, for a horseman was always proud of his
charges, considering them as much his own as of the owner.
He'd *talk* to them all day. There was a bond between them.

HAMES — *tubular rods joined by a bit of leather all resting on the collar*

Then on with the bridle and an ever so heavy collar which helped distribute the load. The HAMES would have the reins threaded through its loops. Chains would then be used to hitch up the implement for the day.

It was usual to have a team of two horses — one male and one female. Ours had names of *Duke & Duchess, Victoria & Albert, Captain & Silver.* To the sound of hooves clopping over the smooth cobbles, he would lead the team out to be watered at the granite trough in the yard. Then it would be off to the fields for a full 12 hour working day.

One task would be ploughing. Everyone associates farming with ploughing. It used to be a long weary job for both the horse and the horseman. All that walking up and down the furrows from dawn until dusk. All the time balancing and driving the plough this way and that. Another task would be rolling. Here the ground is prepared for the seed at Easter. Seeds used then were very different to those used today. It was then not possible to grow such a quantity of grass as we do from the present day seed. The seed used was *Cocksfoot,* similar to much of the grasses still seen on the cliff tops. *White clover* was included as it grew to 3 to 4 inches.

(there is a more modern picture of a Trenuggo pair of shires pulling a roller on page 14)

Honey bees loved that clover. People depended on honey to sweeten their food. Cane sugar was so very expensive. The hay season would follow, with all hands out to turn the cut grass daily, until it was dry enough to be loaded onto a wagon and built into a hayrick nearby.

Whatever the task, all of them would have a break or two. For the horse a nuzzle out of its nosebag. For the horseman, who will have walked as far as his horse, a rest sitting on the hedge crunching his CROUST and admiring their combined handiwork. Then on again until the job was done, or darkness fell, which ever came first.

CROUST — *food taken mid-shift, both morning & afternoon*

Back to the farmyard would come the weary team. The horse would go to the water while the horseman fetched his oil lantern. With shadows flickering from the soft light, he'd call to the horse to come into the stable for the night. Now the horse's job was done but his was still unfinished. There was the routine of removing the harness, putting on the tethering night rope, clearing the hooves and finally a good brush up. Hopefully all would be well next day. A last look to his charges before going to bed. The horseman used to tell me: "A lovely job working with horses you know."

The brasses and leathers would have a good clean and polish at weekends. A favourite time seemed to be Sunday morning before going to church.

The dairyman

Rising at 6:00am, the dairyman would go straight into the cow shed to hand-milk half a dozen cows from his perch on a short three legged stool on the rough floor. The farmer's lad will already have brought the cows around to their stalls, each tethered in place by a leather strap around her neck.

Cows were often named after those flowers in bloom at the occasion of their birth – *Bluebell, Daisy, Poppy & Celandine*. Sometimes the name of a farm, or person from whom she was bought, was used – *Alsia's Mary & Belle of Trendrennen*. Each cow knew her way to her own stall. The pale coloured, placid natured, *Guernsey* was the favourite breed in the Cornwall of the 1900's. Patiently awaiting their milker. The same person would milk the same cow – twice daily. In the winter it could be trying for the dairyman. What with an animal's wet muddy foot knocking over the bucket now and then, or a wet tail swishing about one's face. Hopefully not into the milk bucket! I always remember that golden yellow froth swishing about on top of the warm milk.

except within six weeks of a term, when a cow would be dried off to favour the unborn calf

The *farmyard hunters*, after working the night shift, would now wander in. With a loud *miaowing* announcement they'd make known their demand for a just reward for a night's work!

The milk would be carried off to the farm's dairy to be strained through a fine muslin cloth into ten gallon churns, then all would go back indoors for breakfast – at last.

here are some distant cousins of those cows of the 1900's

Afterwards the men would go off to the farm work and the women to the dairy work. That milk required for the family to drink daily would be put to one side, the rest processed in a hand cranked separator. Beautiful yellow cream would pour out of one spout and the thinner fatless whey out of another. The cream would be poured into a bowl to set further while being stored on the cool of the pantry slate shelf.

Some would be put aside to make into butter, often a difficult task on a hot summer's day. The whey would be fed to the pigs, though a little might be put aside to make pastry or *Hevva* cake. Two days before a market day more cream than usual would be made, for sale along with seasonal farm produce. From here, all this would have been sent to those markets at St. Just and Penzance.

In those bygone years, it was more important hereabouts to live at peace with oneself, than consider what money could be had from farming. Milk would have been the main source of income. However, when one showed friends or callers over one's farm, it was with a sense of pride in the proper appearance of a repaired hedge, healthy looking herds & crops and with the overall cleanliness of the farmyard. Good land management involved weed control by the rotation of crops and many hours with hook & hoe. Nowadays a farmer is more likely to indicate his pride, to those same callers, by quoting the returns and profitabilities of each field or animal.

In the 1900's a dairy farmer would keep a cow on 3 acres. Today's farmer can expect to keep that cow on $^2/_3{}^{rd}$ of an acre – thanks to the modern improved varieties of grass seed.

there are about 2½ acres to a hectare

The milk was usually dealt with on site. Some farmers had small delivery carts. Each farm's household must have breathed a sign of relief when the *cooperative* milk factory was formed at Bottoms. At first it took no milk on Sundays, but practicality soon prevailed. Equally importantly, classes began to help farmers improve dairy parlour hygiene and also to unify production. I have a photograph of Gran sitting proudly at one of these gatherings.

see page 128

In those years, an older child's birthday present was likely to be a milking stool. Three legged ones were the most popular as they could be stood more securely on the uneven floor. The children didn't need to be prompted. This was a privilege and a long awaited cue to join with the grown-ups in the milking. Of course a quiet cow would be allocated.

The pig man

Pigs were often a secondary income. They ate the waste food from the farmhouse, excess turnips etc, and so proved fairly cheap to keep. *Yorkshire Whites* and *Gloucester Spots* were popular in those days.

At mating time it was not uncommon to see a man with a sow, tied by her back leg, walking along the lanes GUIDING her to a neighbour's farm. When the piglets had grown to the required size they would be slaughtered there on the farm. A noose would be flung over the snout and yanked up. Another person would quickly slice through the neck right under the bottom jaw. It would be hung up on a beam, washed in boiling hot water and its coarse hair shaved off. The carcass would be covered with a very white cloth, loaded onto a cart and taken to the butcher for sale. His fee was generally to keep a fifth of the pig and also the valuable LIGHTS.

GUIDING – *a pig can't be pulled along and has to be driven from behind*

LIGHTS – *heart, liver, kidney etc*

The fox, hare & rabbit

Foxes. Lovely to look at and now getting popular with the town folk, especially as it has found easy pickings amongst the back gardens and the almost casually discarded food waste.

I hope this mutual feeling lasts. We country folk know the vixen's regular den and enjoy watching her and the cubs playing in the spring. The loss of the odd lamb or chicken is usually acceptable, but the fox has a habit of leaving the whole hen house massacred but having only taken [eaten] the one. I do not appreciate being left without my egg making machines!

The fox hunt gets rough publicity. It always has been a good social event for the country folk. Always a great sight in the autumn and winter to see the hunt in full cry across our fields. More often now, the hunt consists of riders from the towns taking a day off work. Still whatever, I do feel that the hunt has its place in the overall health of the fox

old picture of the Western Hunt at Buryas Bridge – the Garage's end wall can still be seen over what is now the A30

(Pz to Land's End is from right to left)

community by culling the old and sick foxes. Mr. Thomas [Lower Alsia] had a resident fox that used to lose the hunt every time – by evading them up in one of his haylofts!

Hares. One of our country sports that has been outlawed is hare coursing. This used to be a men's autumn social event. A group of a dozen men, each with a greyhound on a leash, would walk the fields. There was a pre-arranged order of racing. On sighting a hare the next greyhound would be pointed but not unleashed until the hare had run a fair distance. It would be a cardinal sin to release your dog either out of order or early. Mind you, the hare was not intended to be caught by the greyhound. The intent of the sport was just in the fine judging of the *quality of run* against the wiles of the hare!

Joe Murley of Trembothick Farm; my Uncle Pearce's brother

Rabbits. Gone are the days when I would have welcomed a rabbit being given to me by a hunter at the back door, his gun cranked open resting in the crook of his arm – with excited dogs circling at his feet. From St. Buryan the morning bus used to go away to Penzance with open slated crates of two dozen rabbit carcasses, hung by the back legs with the little white tails bobbing out... Also small flower boxes of violets. These two seasonal *cash crops* would be loaded by the bus conductor and this in advance of us walking passengers!

Myxomatosis has seen to all that. It's a very unpleasant virus brought in from France by some over-anxious farmers who wanted something to control rabbits after that population exploded when the *gin-trap* was outlawed. True, the virus did the job, but very few farmers applauded it.

I remember having to swipe swollen headed, pus-ridden, deaf & blind rabbits eating feverishly, in order to put them out of their misery. Sometimes twenty to thirty at a time. Never again I hope. This seems to have changed the lifestyle of rabbit families. Once groups stayed in a particular area for generations. Now you will find a field with no rabbits, then – all of a sudden – overrun for a few weeks at a time, before most of them apparently then move on.

All farmers had dogs (usually terriers or collies) to assist with cattle and with hunting rabbits. A farm's terrier also did help to keep the rat population down.

I remember father knocking rats off the calf shed rafters while I held the Tilley lamp. *Grippo*, our terrier, caught them in mid-air, shook them and they were dead. Afterwards *Grippo* carried out the carcasses and stacked them neatly ready for disposal. No training here mind, it all came naturally to him. I call this kinder than the laying down of chemicals and using other such poisons.

a typical gateway – near Vellansager and looking towards Lamorna

The shepherd

Very few sheep were kept, for a full life-cycle, in this area. More sheep are seen nowadays, though they tend to be just rented in for short grazing seasons to keep the grass down and help with the *nitrogen levels* [more on this next!].

The FYM pile

FYM – *also known*
as farmyard manure

What nutrients are taken out of a field, on a crop being harvested, have to be replaced. The land otherwise becomes infertile. Historically the fields hereabouts were revitalised with a mixture of farmyard manure and seaweed. Nowadays chemical fertilisers are ubiquitous, although the *healthy* aroma of the sluicing of the farmyard slurry tanks can still be found near dairy farms! They still say that if you can smell that, then at least you know you're still alive!

Land preparation has changed radically, it used to be thus:
Soil would be removed from the ditch (cut the width of a *Cornish shovel*), loaded into a cart and dropped at the centre of a field. It would then be covered with salt or seaweed. During the next three years all the manure from the farmyard would be placed on top. Upon the right season and, depending on the crop to follow, this would then be spread all over the field.

1990's FYM heap
here at Alsia Farm,
but there again it
hasn't changed
that much
since the
1900's

Horses were used for all the heavy pulling and carrying on the farm. It was considered a good day's work for a single man and horse team to spread 20 cart loads of this preparation a day. By adding another man to help shovel, 35 cart loads would make a day's work. A low sliding sledge could be worked very much harder. The horse and man team would work as fast as they could, because they knew once this target was reached the rest of the day was their own. Indeed the horse somehow didn't take long to learn that either!

A farmer knew how much to expect of a labourer and most asked no more than they would of themselves. The greater majority had done that work themselves before.

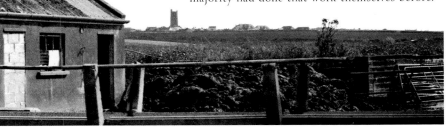

The scythe man

I remember my uncle explaining how the corn was cut by
hand with a scythe:

> A team went forward. Swinging in an everlasting rhythm with
> cut straw flowing off the blades in a sheen of rolling gold.
> Sounding of running water, this flaxen belt came to rest upon
> the ground awaiting the straightening of the follower boys.
> With a light stick they would tap the straw into bigger sections.
> Nine days later a man would make these sections into sheaves.

Eight sheaves would form a sort of tent – called a *shock*.

In changeable weather a choice would be made as to whether
to form protective MOWs quickly right there in the field, or
whether there would be enough time to cart it all over to the
MOWHAY. If there were enough men available an even bigger
KNEE MOW would be made in the field. This was so named as
it was the knee that kept a sheaf in place whilst deciding
where to put the next.

When the weather had settled and the mows or knee mows
dried sufficiently, the final stacking stage would be done.

When the sheaves had completely dried, they would be
carted into that area known as the mowhay, kept well away
from the larger livestock, but near their barns. Great ricks
would be literally built – big as a cottage! The basic
technique was to form an oblong hollow ring of sheaves,
after which the inside would be
methodically filled. Similarly, a
slightly smaller oblong ring would be
built on top and that too filled in.
This continued until there was
nothing on which to build the next
oblong! The rick's basically conical
nature shed the rain – just like a
thatched roof. Any sheaves remaining
would be made into a knee mow.

MOW – *sounds like
'cow' and is formed
with seven shocks*
MOWHAY *(silent 'h')
the part of the yard
for hay & straw*
KNEE MOW – *about
a wagon load
size of mow*

*unknown little boy
helping on the farm
by putting the hay
(here) into 'pooks'*

If made properly it would all keep dry until the following March. The first threshing would be done later in autumn to supply winter grain and would normally fill the barn to capacity. By March the remaining corn would be threshed to replenish stock. This would be when *Grippo* would come into action again, for the rats would have to emerge, panic stricken, from their *winter quarters*! The picture shows my brother Roger and *Grippo* out the back.

The furze man

FURZE — *a bush similar to a gorse bush with a stem of some three feet; the term has become confused with the modern gorse bush*

He would call early to cut FURZE. It was once used for fuel and would be cut into *tashes*, which were convenient bundles layered alternately. Two hundred of these tashes would make a square *faggot* — considered to be a year's supply for a kitchen fireplace. In the autumn he would also cut peat turfs of some 18 inches by 9 inches out of the moorlands.

The seamstress

She would walk miles from one regular employer to the next, carrying her heavy sewing machine in one hand and home-made carpetbag in the other. Her work would keep her there for four or five days at a time, working from the end of the kitchen table making new or repairing any of the household's requirements. The mistress of the household would find a room for her seamstress and she would usually become a temporary member of the family. How times have changed. Just consider how you would treat someone similarly offering *live-in home services*!

The threshing man

Perhaps the man that caused the most excitement, if not the most work, noise and dust for the whole year!

Us children would be out waiting to hear him coming from afar, ever closer...

twin Margaret & I — out waiting!

The farmers would have already arranged the order he would service each farm. A room would be prepared in the servant's quarters. On his arrival (usually late evening) he would get his threshing machine lined up beside the rick in the mowhay and test the belts rolling. There must be no hold ups. It'll be a long day's work for some 16 men who will have congregated from neighbouring farms. These men would come from their farms and the work returned, in kind, on their turn.

The threshing day would start early. All the men would arrive soon after they'd had breakfast and the thresher man would already have *steam up* on the traction engine and be rolling the belts. It would be a very very dusty and heavy day's work. Sheaves would be forked over to the thresher man on top; the resulting grain sacked and manhandled into the empty waiting barns. The *thrashed* straw bundles, ready tied by the machinery, restacked in the mowhay. By the end of the day the rick would have appeared to have *walked* from one side of the threshing machine to the other!

There would be two croust breaks and also a *dinner* [lunch]. During these the traction engine would steam quietly but the noisy rattle of the threshing machine would be stilled. Now the stories and gossip could be passed about! Our men would eat and drink well. For the crousts they would be treated with full white linen lined croust baskets laden with hevva cake, seed cake, 'saffi' cake, fresh splits and jam sandwiches. This would be washed down with fresh ground coffee no less, brought out in great enamelled jugs – also large black kettles of tea. With all the food on the ground in the baskets I never saw one dog steal. They would naturally wait to be thrown something tasty.

1900's threshing – as Mr. F.W. Alford & 'Meg' demonstrate at the 'Preservation'

As you already know, *Grippo* would be ready on duty – waiting for emerging rats. Midday they would have a *sit down* roast, with three or four vegetables, back in the farmhouse kitchen. Everything piled high, apple tarts with Cornish cream, all followed by plates of cake. No stinting in those days…

The blacksmith

He was the man that everyone went to for a repair of anything metallic – be it pipe work, cisterns, farm machinery, JINGLES and, of course, for shoeing the horses.

JINGLE – *this is a little cart used for social events*

Almost gone is the sound of the *tap tap tap clunk* at the anvil and the acrid smell of hooves scorching. It would also be the men's meeting house for a chat on the latest local happenings, while waiting for a piece of equipment to be welded or otherwise tapped into shape, so to last for another season.

The picture shows blacksmiths from all around at the opening of Messrs. Males' new *shop* at St. Buryan [1953]. Areas that were represented [top left & then working clockwise]: *Gulval, St. Buryan, Newmill, Camborne, Newmill, Penzance, St. Ives (2), St. Erth, Gerry Male, Penzance, St. Just, Hayle and finally — Gerry & Ken Male's father* [*no Ken… perhaps he was inside already working?*]

Farming today

HEMP — *paper, rope & cloth (not the drug)* STINGING NETTLES *— for wines & ropes!*

Alsia Farm — with flax growing in the foreground; that is St. Buryan Church in the distance

Farming is always changing. At present there is an abundance of food that is being imported cheaper than can be home produced. It has meant that other crops have had to be considered, so that livelihoods can continue here in the countryside. The land must remain in good condition for when it may once again be needed to feed our own. There is an increase in the growing of linseed both for its oil, which is mixed with other ingredients to make fodder for cattle, and for the straw which is being otherwise developed in the textile, geotextile, agrotextile, paper and automotive industries. Flax is being reintroduced and has provided material for some of the finest garments in the fashion industry. Other new or more fashionable crops include HEMP, STINGING NETTLES and various environmentally sensitive items. In a search for low input biomass crops several types of long grass have been developed. On burning, these fast growing products release only that CO_2 absorbed in growth and thus is not a contributory factor for the *greenhouse effect*. Similarly there is a willow type crop to be burnt for power generation. It would be too easy to forget the old ways in these days of intensive farming.

Some of the old ways should be preserved!

The *Preservation*

A very popular annual July family event held at the village of St. Buryan. People arrive to show off their *pride and joy*, all keen to tell you of the repairs and renovations made.

Engines of all kinds – tiny water-pumping donkey engines up to the monstrous traction engines. Motorcycles, motorcars and trucks – very early up to not quite vintage. Tractors – the

the steam traction engine "Prosper" & trusting friend

slight crop weeder of the *Allis Chalmer* mould, right up to the great heavy workhorse *Oliver* or *Fordson*. The Western Hunt always attend and the children are invited into the ring to meet their well-mannered hounds. Each year a theme is chosen and there is always a jovial guest speaker 'hanging off' the Tannoy system to keep you informed and amused whilst you watch from your *Grandstand seats* [straw bales]. Wandering into the exhibition marquee, you will see displays of country crafts, hand tools and collections of old models, bottles and such like. It is incredible how such a small community can, in a wholly voluntary capacity, organise such a popular event with so much interest – year after year.

The Handicraft & Horticultural Show

Many such shows are held throughout the country. I feel that our July show in St. Buryan has been adversely affected by our smaller farms being amalgamated and the ever increasing number of retired folk settling amongst us who haven't yet caught the *showing bug*. In times past it was with great excitement & neighbourly rivalry that the show blossomed. There are vegetable, summer fruits, flower, photography, cookery, sewing classes – in fact the gamut of handicrafts and horticultural skills.

Epilogue

I do hope you have enjoyed your **Safari West** in this my own dear area of Cornwall. So too, sharing with me those little happenings along life's way which, at any time, may strike in awe, in surprise or in humour.

Appendix

Illustration acknowledgements

I would very much like to thank the following, all of whom contributed so generously to the success of **Safari West**:

Page	Subject	Contributor
(front)	*Averil, Henry and Milton*	*MH*
(back)	*Penrose ghost story*	*RH*
(pref)	*compass*	*RH*
(pref)	*map*	*RH*
(pref)	*Boscawen Point watercolour*	*Rosemary Harlow*
9	*Lamorna Cove*	*MH*
11	*Rev. Spry cartoon sketch*	*David Reames*
12	*tree sketches*	*Liz Rich*
13	*'First & Last' Garage*	*Bryan Roberts*
14	*Shire horses at Trenuggo*	*RH*
15	*map*	*RH*
16	*map*	*RH*
16	*Vellansager*	*RH*
18	*St. Buryan Chapel*	*MH*
19	*Band of Hope procession*	*Valerie Humphrys*
21	*St. Buryan tower sketch*	*Liz Rich*
22	*grasses*	
22	*barn owl sketch*	*Liz Rich*
23	*daffodil sketch*	*Liz Rich*
24	*snowed up mill*	*MH*
25	*river threesome*	*MH*
26	*Alsia well*	*RH*
27	*Penrose (modern)*	*RH*
28	*ship*	
28	*pebbled beach*	*RH*
29	*Whitesand Bay*	*RH*
31	*Whitesand beach at Sennen Cove*	*RH*
34	*Penrose (ghost story)*	*RH*
38	*ship*	
39	*The Tribbens*	*Bryan Roberts*
41	*Trevilley*	*RH*
42	*Penberth river*	*RH*
43	*map and icons*	*RH*
46	*overmantle* (by kind permission Mrs F. Hosking)	*RH*

On the name of Alsia

(very locally) this
sounds like ail-leah

Over the years many have asked me about the name of Alsia.
In this area most of the older places can be traced to people
or the other way around. So I include these little pieces of
knowledge from my old notes so that those, who would wish
to seek further into the past, may have a lead to follow.

When reading old English do remember to read the 'f' as an 's'!

From the *Magna Britannia Vol III Cornwall - Gulval* [7]

includes Churchtown,
Chyendower,
Trevarrack & Trezela

The manor of Laneftley or Lanifley, which was formerly the
name of the Parish belonged at an early period to the family of
De Als, who took their name from the manor of Alfa or Als, in
the parish of St. Buryan.

It goes on to say the De Als family gave the mentioned manor
at Gulval to the priory of St. Germans in 1266.

that is to say, this
parish of Gulval
near Penzance

This manor of Laneseley in this parish, was in the time of
Richard I and King John, the lands of the family surnamed
De Als, now Hals, so called from the barton and dismantled
manor of Als, now Alse and Alesa, in Buryan, as tradition saith, or
Beer Alseton, Alston in Devon, in impossession of Trevassion and
others, whereof they were Lords; & in particular William de Als,
in the beginning of the reign of King Henry III that married
Mary the daughter of Francis de Bray, was posseded thereof;
Father of Simon de Alls, who lived at Halsham in Yorkshire
(from his denominated), that married Jane, daughter of
Thomas de Campo Arnulpho (now Champernown); Sheriff of
York 2nd, 3rd, 6th and 7th years of King Henry III 1222 A.D.
As appears from the catalogue of those sheriffs, and the Hal's
allowed pedigree 1483 from which also it is manifest, by an
authentic deed or record therein, yet legible that the said Simon
for the health and salvation of his soul, his wife's and ancestors'
and other relations', gave the said manor of Laneseley to the
Prior of St. Germans... their successors... for ever...

Other historical 'gems'

These rough draft notes may be of interest to a student.

From the *Cornish Church Guide* [10]   (*page 20*)

...in the year 909 Edward the Elder founded a bishopric for Devonshire, with its See at Crediton, and annexed to it three towns in Cwll, Pawton, Callington and Lawhitton, to be missionary centres from which Eadulf might annually visit the Cornish people who still persisted in their opposition to the English and Roman discipline. The mission of Eadulf and the arms of Athelstan finally incorporated the Cornish into the English Church. Conan, the native Cornish Bishop, appears as a member of Athelstan's WITENAGEMOT from A.D. 931, and Cornwall was thenceforward an English Diocese.

Continuing from the *Cornish Church Guide* [10]   (*page 25*)

...it remained for King Athelstan in 930 to achieve the complete political and religious conquest of Cornwall. As Lord of Cornwall, from Land's End to the Tamar in a fuller sense than any of his predecessors, he was able to plant a Saxon bishopric a step nearer – viz at St. Germans. The bishop appointed to the newly formed Diocese of Cornwall bore the Celtic name of Conan.

Continuing from the *Cornish Church Guide* [10]   (*page 67*)

...the ecclesiastical history of St Buryan (properly Beryan) is curious and interesting. Circa 930 King Athelstan established a College of Secular Canons here on the site of the hermitage of St. Beriana, endowing it with extensive lands in the parish. By 1085, though reduced in extent, they still belonged to the Church.

...in 1238 Bishop Briwere seems to have re-established the College when he re-dedicated the church in honour of the B.V.M., S.S. Andrew Apostle, Thomas the Martyr, Nicholas & Beriana.

The College consisted of a dean and three prebendaries and, down to A.D.1300, the visitorial rights of the bishops were exercised without objection and the deans installed by them – on the presentation of the Earls of Cwll. On the death of Earl Edmund the earldom escheated to King Edward I and, for the first time, claims were advanced as to the church being a Royal Free Chapel outside episcopal jurisdiction. This notion was really an ingenious fabrication of a pluralist whom the King had presented to the deanery and who wished it to be proved a sinecure. A long and

a predecessor is the Diocesan Kalendar [11]

Eadulf was a newly appointed bishop

describes us Cornish sure enough, we hate being dictated to!

WITENAGEMOT – *the king's judicial advisors*

documents and tradition tell us that he also reconstituted the monasteries at Probus & St. Buryan

(*note that Probus & St. Buryan have the two tallest church towers in Cornwall*)

bitter struggle ensued between the Crown and the Diocesans. Bishop Grandisson obtained a momentary victory when he visited Buryan in triumph on 12th July 1336, to absolve the repentant clergy and parishioners from sentence of excommunication. Accompanied by three knights, two archdeacons, many prelates and a multitude of clergy the great bishop received their submission – delivering in Latin an appropriate sermon which the rector of St. Just interpreted in Cornish and others in English and French. In the end however, the Crown triumphed and we hear no more of episcopal interference at Buryan.

bet my ancestors froze to the ground when they saw that lot enter the village

The deanery became a Royal Donative and all episcopal rights were excluded. By ℭ the dean and three prebendaries were all habitually nonresident and their places taken by curates. The latter served the church and the parochial chapels of Sennen and St. Levan then belonging to it. The 100 Masses which, under Athelstan's Charter were bound to be said for the souls of the Kings of England, were performed by a chantry priest. In 1545 the establishment consisted of 13 persons; the nonresident deans and three prebendaries, the three curates, the King's priest, three clerks as proxies for the prebendaries and two layman – viz: the steward and official peculiar of the deanery who proved wills and kept the deanery courts. Under the Act of 1545 the prebends were abolished but the deanery survived until 1864, when it was split up into the three rectories of St. Buryan, St. Levan and Sennen. It is possible that there was no dean resident after ℭ .

Carnmeal was the ancient name of that hill; suggests dedication to the archangel

Continuing from the *Cornish Church Guide* [10]   *(page 114)*
...among other chapels in the parish may be named those traditionally dedicated to St. Helen at Cape Cornwall and to St. Michael on Chapel Carn Brea.

Continuing from the *Cornish Church Guide* [10]   *(page 142)*
...St. Levan (St. Selevan) brother of St. Just enlarged in the ℭ ...font from the first period ...excellent woodwork from the second period.

Continuing from the *Cornish Church Guide* [10]   *(page 194)*
...Sennen. Until 1864 Sennen and St. Levan were but chapels to the deanery of Buryan. Sennen only acquired rights of sepulture in 1430 – by application to the Pope. In 1440 the church, having been rebuilt, was reconsecrated in honour of St. John Baptist – as appears from an inscription at the base of the font.

In 1327, the free-for-all brawl took place in the churchyard, blood spilt, and bishop Walter of Exeter pronounced the Greater Excommunication against * of the parishioners who had sided with the King. Some of the names mentioned: Vivian & Joceus Penrose – Sennen; Richard and his sons William & Hugh Vyvyans of Trevedran – St. Buryan.

* I found several references ranging from 11 up to 43

and it continues; that on 4th November 1328...

Richard Vyvyan and his sons William & Hugh were excommunicated with other men of St. Buryan by the bishop in the chapel of the priory of St. Michael's Mount. They had assaulted Richard de Beaupre, the rector of St. Just in the churchyard.

from the Trelowarren house prospectus: 'Vyvyans of Trevidranor or Treviddren' (now Trevedran)

The bishop of Exeter blew out the lights and he said:

As these lights in our bodily sight are thus extinguished, so in the presence of God and the Blessed Mary and the Blessed Angel and all Saints are these persons extinguished spiritually and delivered to the Devil and his Angels to be punished in eternal fire unless they are penitent and come to their right senses.

William was the only Vyvyan who was subsequently absolved on 12th July 1336.

Bibliography

[1]   *"The Old Stones of Land's End"* by J. Michell

[2]   *"Methodism in St. Buryan"* by J.M. Hosking

[3]   OS map (1908) 2nd edition – Baker's Downs

[4]   *"Traditions and Hearthside Stories of West Cornwall"* by W. Bottrell

[5]   *"Essays in Cornish History"* by Charles Henderson

[6]   *"Civil war in Cornwall"* by M. Coates

[7]   *"Magna Britannia Vol III Cornwall - Gulval"* (printed 1814)

[8]   Taylor's book – I haven't been able to trace this one; if a reader might know of it, I'd certainly appreciate the details!

[9]   *"Watchers on the Longships"* by J. F. Cobb F.R.G.S.

[10]   *"Cornish Church Guide"* – preface Walterus Truron (printed by Oscar Blackford 1925)

[11]   *"Diocesan Kalendar"* – appearance year by year in a booklet or catalogue form

[12]   *"Visitation of Cwll"* – by various and collation by Lieutenant Colonel J. L. Vivian

My appreciation goes to those helpful people at the Penzance Library (Morrab Gardens).

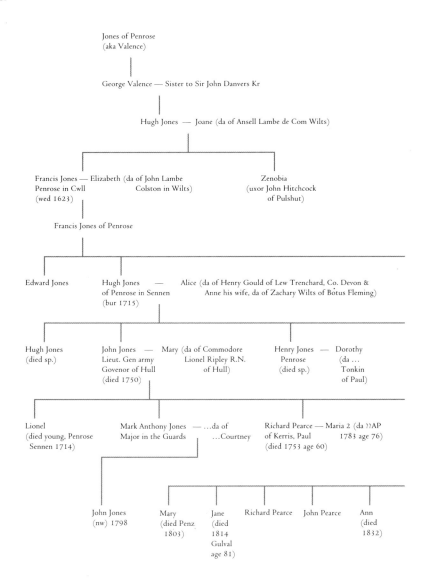

Jones of Penrose
(aka Valence)

George Valence — Sister to Sir John Danvers Kr

Hugh Jones — Joane (da of Ansell Lambe de Com Wilts)

Francis Jones — Elizabeth (da of John Lambe   Zenobia
Penrose in Cwll   Colston in Wilts)   (uxor John Hitchcock
(wed 1623)   of Pulshut)

Francis Jones of Penrose

Edward Jones   Hugh Jones   —   Alice (da of Henry Gould of Lew Trenchard, Co. Devon &
                      of Penrose in Sennen   Anne his wife, da of Zachary Wilts of Botus Fleming)
                      (bur 1715)

Hugh Jones   John Jones   —   Mary (da of Commodore   Henry Jones   —   Dorothy
(died sp.)   Lieut. Gen army   Lionel Ripley R.N.   Penrose   (da ...
                    Govenor of Hull   of Hull)   (died sp.)   Tonkin
                    (died 1750)   of Paul)

Lionel   Mark Anthony Jones — ...da of   Richard Pearce — Maria 2 (da ??AP
(died young, Penrose   Major in the Guards   ...Courtney   of Kerris, Paul   1783 age 76)
Sennen 1714)   (died 1753 age 60)

John Jones   Mary   Jane   Richard Pearce   John Pearce   Ann
(nw) 1798   (died Penz   (died   (died
                    1803)   1814   1832)
                                   Gulval
                                   age 81)

The Jones ancestry traced
in the "Visitation of Cwll"
(page 245)

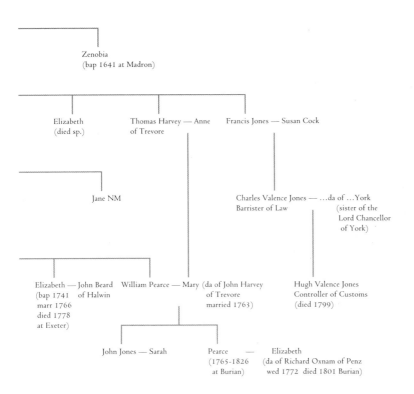

Zenobia
(bap 1641 at Madron)

Elizabeth
(died sp.)

Thomas Harvey — Anne
of Trevore

Francis Jones — Susan Cock

Jane NM

Charles Valence Jones — ...da of ...York
Barrister of Law   (sister of the
                    Lord Chancellor
                    of York)

Elizabeth — John Beard   William Pearce — Mary (da of John Harvey
(bap 1741   of Halwin   of Trevore
marr 1766   married 1763)
died 1778
at Exeter)

Hugh Valence Jones
Controller of Customs
(died 1799)

John Jones — Sarah   Pearce   —   Elizabeth
                      (1765-1826   (da of Richard Oxnam of Penz
                      at Burian)   wed 1772 died 1801 Burian)

About the author

The author was born (one of twins) on Alsia Farm and attended the local primary school and the Cape Cornwall Comprehensive, later joining the Brush End School at Lelant, finishing up at Penwith Commercial College.

As a youngster Mary was a keen member of the Young Farmers Club – later an enthusiastic member of the Women's Institute and the W.R.V.S.

She married and is now back at Alsia where she runs the farm with the help of her family of two daughters and five sons.

A busy lady, Mary still finds time for her tapestries, as exemplified by the church kneelers she has completed. She also paints and enjoys writing!

PHOTOGRAPH BY THE TED FORD STUDIO, PENZANCE, CORNWALL.